"Every time I opened this book, I felt like I was sitting with a trusted friend who pointed me back to Christ. *Let Him In* isn't just a devotional. It's a gentle daily reminder that the Savior is with me, even on the quiet days."
—Jessica T., North Carolina

"*Let Him In* is exactly the kind of devotional I've been looking for—short enough for busy mornings, deep enough to stir my soul, and always centered on Christ. I've never felt so spiritually steady."
—Emily W., St. George, Utah

"As a Latter-day Saint woman trying to stay anchored in the gospel, I've found this book to be one of my most cherished resources. Each entry speaks truth, encourages action, and helps me feel closer to the Savior."
—Sarah M., Alberta, Canada

"Some devotionals are good. This one is sacred. *Let Him In* helps me see Christ in my everyday life. It's helped me see the holy in the ordinary."
—Rebecca L., Coeur d'Alene, Idaho

"I love how actionable this book is. It's not just sweet thoughts, it's real discipleship. It helps me listen to the Spirit, act in faith, and stay rooted in what really matters."

—Nathan K., Phoenix, Arizona

"I can feel Emmaline's testimony on every page. This is clearly a labor of love. Her words are thoughtful, humble, and full of light. *Let Him In* is a book I'll be gifting to friends for years to come."

—Ana M., São Paulo, Brazil

"If you need a devotional that is Christ-centered, scripture-based, and completely uplifting, this is the one. *Let Him In* has helped me build a daily habit of turning to the Lord."

—James F., London, England

Let Him In

LET HIM IN; Daily Devotionals to Hear Him, Follow Him, and Become Like Him Copyright © 2025 / First edition by Emmaline Hoffmeister

All rights reserved.

No portion of this book may be reproduced, distributed, or transmitted in any form or by any means, including photocopying, recording, or other electronic or mechanical methods, without the prior written permission of the publisher, except in the case of brief quotations embodied in critical reviews and certain other noncommercial uses permitted by U.S. copyright law.

The mention of songs and scripture included in this work are the property of their respective songwriters and copyright holders. They are used here for creative purposes under fair use, and no infringement is intended. All rights to these songs remain with their original creators and are referenced in the endnotes. All scripture references in this work are taken from the King James Version of the Holy Bible and the standard works of The Church of Jesus Christ of Latter-day Saints, including the Book of Mormon, the Doctrine and Covenants, the Pearl of Great Price, and other standard church works.

ISBNs
eBook: 978-1-936850-33-4
Paperback: 978-1-936850-39-6

Jacket, cover, and interior design by Emmaline Hoffmeister
Editing by PWA Editing Services
Cover image © Adobe Firefly: "Jesus Christ knocking on an old door in Jerusalem. Summer."
Fonts AT Avalaqus Serif, Garamond, EB Garamond, and My Soul
Author photo © MJ Hodges Photography

For permissions requests, write to the publisher at:
Rhemalda Publishing
c/o Author Emmaline Hoffmeister
101 Rainbow Dr. #9867, Livingston, TX 77399

Let Him In

The chapel was quiet as Michael stood to bear his testimony. It had been years since he had spoken at a pulpit, but today something stirred in him.

"I had a dream," he began, his voice steady. "In it, I saw Jesus Christ standing outside a door. He was knocking, gently but firmly. I saw His face. I knew it was Him. I felt peace, urgency, and love all at once. But I didn't know what it meant."

Michael paused, the memory vivid. "A few weeks later, I met two missionaries. They asked if they could share a message. I almost said no, but something told me to listen. At our first meeting, I was prompted to tell them about my dream. They listened and then showed me a painting. It was the Savior, standing at a door with no handle, gently knocking."

He looked around the congregation, eyes misting. "It was the exact image from my dream."

"The painting was *Jesus at the Door* by Del Parson. It depicts Christ knocking on the door of our hearts. The handle is only on the inside. He never forces His way in. He waits. He knocks. But we must choose to open the door."

"That dream," Michael said softly, "was Christ calling me home. And those missionaries helped me open the door."

A quiet reverence filled the chapel. In that moment, Michael wasn't just telling a story. He was testifying of a Savior who seeks, who waits, who knocks, always with love.

May 29th

The day I wrote this devotional, it felt like the Spirit had written it for me first. Every word reminded me of what I personally needed to hear. It was as if the Lord had whispered comfort into my heart, then asked me to share it. I did not realize until afterward that I was the first one ministered to.

Introduction

Dearest Reader,

This book began with a sacred assignment. It was clear from the beginning that the Lord had something specific in mind. It was not to be just a collection of thoughts, but a spiritual companion to guide hearts day by day. Writing each devotional became a journey of discipleship. As I studied, pondered, and prayed, I found myself strengthened and renewed.

Each page was written with intention. The Lord's hand was present in the process, guiding the words and shaping the messages. I witnessed His goodness, His timing, and His deep desire to bless His children. The devotionals in this book were not written out of lack, but out of a desire to draw closer to Him and to help others do the same.

This has been a labor of love and a stewardship I felt called to complete. If the words here lift you, strengthen you, or help you see the Savior more clearly, then the purpose of this book has been fulfilled.

All My Love,
Emmaline

How to Use This Book

This book was designed as a daily devotional companion, with one entry for each day of the year, including a special message for leap year. Each devotional follows a pattern: a verse of scripture or quote, a short reflection, a gentle invitation to act or reflect, and a personal question to ponder or journal about.

You can use it in a number of ways:

- **Daily Reading:** Begin your morning with a devotional to center your thoughts on Christ. Or close the day with one to reflect and find peace.

- **Study Tool:** Use the scripture or quote as a study prompt. Look it up in context, cross-reference it, and write impressions in your journal.

- **Prayer Guide:** Let the daily message shape your prayers. Ask the Lord to help you apply the principle in your own life.

- **Small Group Discussion:** These devotionals work well as conversation starters in families, ministering visits, or group settings.

- **Seasonal Use:** If you don't read every day, follow the themes by month. Each month's focus offers a unique layer of discipleship and growth.

This book is not meant to be rushed. Let each entry be a quiet moment between you and the Lord. Read slowly. Reflect deeply. Return often.

You are not alone in your journey. The Savior walks with you, and His Spirit will guide you as you invite Him into your daily rhythm. May this book be a tool to help you hear Him, trust Him, and rejoice in Him, one day at a time.

January

Begin with Christ as you embrace fresh starts and rediscover your divine identity in Him.

January 1

> *"Therefore if any man be in Christ, he is a new creature: old things are passed away; behold, all things are become new."*
> 2 Corinthians 5:17

NEW CALENDARS, FRESH PLANNERS, hopeful resolutions. There's something sacred about new beginnings. While the world rushes to redefine itself with checklists, the gospel reminds us that transformation comes through Jesus Christ.

In Him, we're not just improving; we're becoming. He makes us new, even in the worn parts: the doubts, the guilt, the fear. Christ never required perfection. He just asks for a heart willing to try again.

Say you've set a goal to read your scriptures each morning. You picture peaceful starts, quiet study, meaningful insights. But life happens: a sick child, a missed alarm, a day that simply gets away from you. Don't quit. Pray. Let the Lord remind you: this isn't about perfection. It's about relationship. Keep turning to Him.

Let this year begin not with pressure, but with peace. You don't need to reinvent yourself. Just return to the One who already knows exactly who you are.

Today, invite Christ into your new year. Pray to see yourself the way He sees you: worthy and capable.

What does it mean to "be in Christ"? How can you let Him shape your fresh start this year?

January 2

> *"I can do all things through Christ which strengtheneth me."*
>
> Philippians 4:13

There's a quiet kind of courage that comes from knowing who you are, and whose you are. When life demands more than your natural capacity, it's easy to feel overwhelmed. But when your identity is rooted in Christ, you tap into strength far beyond your own.

You're not just trying harder. You're drawing power from a divine source.

Think of a time when you started something new; a job, a responsibility at church or in the community, a fitness goal, a healing process. On day one, you might feel unsure. Maybe even afraid. But if you begin with Christ, you don't walk in alone. You bring with you divine backing. A strength that steadies. A peace that stays. And a Savior who believes in you even when you don't yet believe in yourself.

You don't have to be fearless to move forward. You just need faith that Christ goes with you.

Today, when something feels too big, pause and say, "I can do this through Christ." Lean into Him for your strength.

What's something in your life right now that feels bigger than you? How might beginning it with Christ change the outcome?

January 3

> *"Ye are the light of the world. A city that is set on a hill cannot be hid."*
>
> Matthew 5:14

There's a reason Christ called His disciples "the light of the world." Light doesn't try to be seen, it just is. When you know who you are in Christ, you stop trying to prove your worth and start simply reflecting Him.

You weren't meant to blend in or shrink back. You were meant to shine.

But shining doesn't always mean being loud or noticed. Sometimes it looks like kindness in a tense moment. A quiet integrity in a compromising world. A willingness to forgive when it would be easier to hold a grudge. Light shows up in simple, Christlike ways, and it changes everything around it.

You carry His name. That identity matters. You don't have to be perfect to reflect Him. You just have to be willing to let His light through the cracks.

Today, be conscious of the light you carry. Let it shine in one small but intentional way.

When have you felt Christ's light shine through you, even in small or quiet ways?

January 4

> *"Draw nigh to God, and he will draw nigh to you ..."*
>
> James 4:8

Starting with Christ doesn't require a dramatic change of scenery. It begins in the heart. Sometimes we expect a fresh start to look like a grand reset, but often it's something quieter: a whisper of desire to be closer to Him, a simple decision to pray with more intent, a humble turning of the heart.

Christ is always closer than we think. He doesn't wait for us at the finish line. He walks beside us from the first step. The distance we feel is often just distraction, not departure. He never moves away from us. But He always honors even the smallest move we make toward Him.

One woman said she started her mornings with a quiet prayer from bed. Not long, not polished. Just honest. "Help me feel near to Thee today." That little prayer didn't change her schedule, but it changed her soul.

Christ draws near to those who seek Him. He always has. He always will.

Today, reach out in some small, sincere way to draw closer to Christ. He'll meet you there.

What does "drawing near to God" look like in your life right now? How can you take one small step toward Him today?

January 5

> *"Yea, come unto Christ, and be perfected in him, and deny yourselves of all ungodliness; and if ye shall deny yourselves of all ungodliness, and love God with all your might, mind and strength, then is his grace sufficient for you, that by his grace ye may be perfect in Christ; and if by the grace of God ye are perfect in Christ, ye can in nowise deny the power of God."*
>
> Moroni 10:32

The invitation is simple: "Come unto Christ." It's not a one-time gesture. It's a daily choice.

Becoming perfected in Him isn't about flawlessness. When we surrender pride, comparison, and fear, we make space for His grace. He doesn't ask us to do it all. He asks us to let Him in.

One young man, focused on one question each morning: "How can I come unto Christ today?" Some days, it meant offering forgiveness. Other days, it meant saying a more sincere prayer. But always, it brought peace.

You don't have to come all at once. He'll meet you on your path.

Today, ask yourself how you can come unto Christ in one small, meaningful way, and then do it.

What is something you can lay aside in order to come closer to Christ today?

January 6

> *"Look unto me in every thought; doubt not, fear not."*
>
> Doctrine and Covenants 6:36

Some thoughts build faith. Others chip away at it. In the quiet corners of our minds, our identity is constantly being shaped by what we choose to dwell on. That's why the Savior's invitation to "look unto me in every thought" is so powerful. It's not just counsel, it's protection.

Fear thrives when Christ is forgotten. Doubt grows in the absence of truth. But when we deliberately fix our thoughts on Him—His love, His promises, His grace—something shifts. Our hearts steady. Our courage returns.

One sister said she trained her thoughts by whispering "Look to Christ" anytime she felt overwhelmed. It wasn't magic, but it was mindful. And over time, those small spiritual redirects shaped her whole day.

You become what you consistently think about. So think of Him.

Today, catch your thoughts. When fear or doubt creeps in, pause and look to Christ instead.

What recurring thoughts do you want to surrender to Christ? How can you make Him the center of your mental focus today?

January 7

> *"For behold, this is my work and my glory—to bring to pass the immortality and eternal life of man."*
>
> Moses 1:39

From the beginning, God's focus has been clear: you. Your immortality. Your eternal life. You aren't a footnote in His plan. You are the purpose of it.

It's easy to get lost in to-do lists and expectations, even spiritual ones. But God's ultimate goal isn't that you merely check boxes. It's that you come home to Him changed, healed, whole. Everything Christ offers—grace, commandments, covenants, the Spirit—is meant to shape you into who you were always meant to become.

One woman said that realizing "she was God's work" changed how she viewed her life. Instead of trying to prove her worth, she started to live from a place of knowing she had it.

Your life is not random. Your soul is not an accident. You are the focus of a divine and eternal work.

Today, remember that you are God's work and His glory. Live like someone who matters to Him, because you do.

How does knowing God's work is to bring about *your* eternal life change how you see yourself?

January 8

> "You are a child of God. He is the father of your spirit. Spiritually you are of noble birth, the offspring of the King of Heaven."
> Elder Tad R. Callister

There's something steadying about remembering where you come from. Not your hometown or your last name, but your eternal origin. You were born of heavenly parents, and that divine identity is the foundation of everything else.

The world will try to define you by your mistakes, your résumé, your appearance, or your popularity. But God defines you by your lineage: you are His.

Tad R. Callister's reminder is more than poetic. It's revelatory. When you know you're the child of a King, you begin to live like it. You walk with more purpose. You speak with more kindness. You forgive more freely. You stop striving to earn worth and start living from it.

You don't have to prove your divine identity. You just have to remember it.

Today, pause and reflect on your divine heritage. Let that truth shape how you see yourself and how you treat others.

How does knowing you are a child of God influence your choices, your confidence, and your relationships?

January 9

> *"True disciples of Jesus Christ are peacemakers."*
> President Russell M. Nelson

There's something deeply Christlike about choosing peace when the world invites conflict. As a new year unfolds, many set goals to become more productive or successful, but what if the goal was simply to become more like the Prince of Peace?

Being a peacemaker doesn't mean silence. It means presence. It means being anchored enough in Christ that you don't react from fear, but respond with faith. It means seeing others as He sees them, even when they frustrate you. Especially when they frustrate you.

A young man once decided that his goal for the year wasn't to read more or do more, but to *be more*. More forgiving. More gentle. More like Christ. He said, "It wasn't always easy, but it always felt right." And little by little, peace followed him into places it hadn't been before.

You are never more Christlike than when you choose to bring peace where it's needed most.

Today, commit to being a peacemaker. Begin by asking the Lord where your influence could calm, heal, or soften.

In what relationship or setting could you become more of a peacemaker through Christ's help?

January 10

> *"And now, my beloved brethren, I would that ye should come unto Christ, who is the Holy One of Israel, and partake of his salvation, and the power of his redemption ..."*
>
> Omni 1:26

When beginning something new—a goal, a day, a year—it's easy to focus on output. What can I do? How much can I accomplish? But *coming unto Christ* is about input. It is where your soul is nourished and where your strength comes from.

The prophet Amaleki didn't list qualifications. He simply invited: *come*. No matter how far you've wandered, the Savior welcomes you. His arms are open. His salvation is real.

One woman returned to church after years away. She expected judgment but felt peace. "It was as if Christ had been waiting by the door the whole time," she said.

Christ never stops inviting. The fresh start you need begins the moment you turn to Him.

Today, reflect on what it means to "partake of His salvation." Let that shape your focus and your faith.

What might be holding you back from coming fully unto Christ? How can you take one step closer today?

January 11

"Jesus saith unto him, I am the way, the truth, and the life: no man cometh unto the Father, but by me."

John 14:6

In a world overflowing with paths, opinions, and self-made philosophies, Christ makes it clear, He is the way. Not *one* way among many. *The* way. That's not meant to restrict you; it's meant to anchor you.

When you begin with Christ, you don't have to wander in uncertainty. His life is the pattern. His words are the guide. His love is the safety net when you fall short. And because He walked every hard road first, He knows how to walk it with you now.

One young adult said that deciding to follow Christ in every aspect of life didn't make things easier, but it did make things clearer. "I stopped chasing approval and started seeking alignment," she said. "That changed everything."

Christ offers more than direction. He offers transformation. He doesn't just show you the path. He walks it with you and makes you new along the way.

Today, commit to follow *the* way. Ask in prayer how He would have you walk through the decisions you face.

What part of your life most needs Christ's guidance? What would it look like to let Him lead?

January 12

> *"Remember the worth of souls is great in the sight of God;"*
> Doctrine and Covenants 18:10

Before you set another goal or try to become better, pause and remember this truth: *you already matter.* You don't have to earn your worth. God declared it long before you ever took your first breath.

He sees you with eternal eyes. Not as a work in progress or a list of flaws, but as someone of infinite value. Right now. Just as you are.

One young woman shared how this verse became her anchor during a time of deep insecurity. Every time she started to spiral into self-criticism, she'd repeat the phrase: "My worth is great in His sight." Over time, the words stopped being just comforting. They became true.

Beginning with Christ means beginning from a place of worth, not worry. You are already loved. Already seen. Already known.

Today, repeat this truth aloud: "My worth is great in the sight of God." Let that shape your goals and soften your negative self-talk.

In what ways might believing in your divine worth change how you approach today?

January 13

> *"I, the Lord, will forgive whom I will forgive,
> but of you it is required to forgive all men."*
> Doctrine and Covenants 64:10

Forgiveness is one of the most Christlike things we're asked to do, and sometimes one of the hardest. It's not always about the other person. Often, it's about freeing yourself from the burden of bitterness.

Christ never asked us to forget the pain or pretend it didn't matter. He asked us to trust Him with it. To place the injustice, the misunderstanding, the betrayal in His hands, and let Him carry it.

One man said that when he finally chose to forgive, the situation hadn't changed. But he had. The weight he had carried for years lifted, and in its place came peace. It wasn't immediate. But it was real.

Forgiveness doesn't excuse what happened. It simply allows Christ to heal what was wounded.

Today, ask the Lord to help you begin the process of forgiving someone, even if it is only in your heart. Let Him take it from there.

Is there someone you need to forgive so you can move forward with peace? How can Christ help you take that first step?

January 14

> *"Learn of me, and listen to my words; walk in the meekness of my Spirit, and you shall have peace in me."*
>
> Doctrine and Covenants 19:23

Peace is one of the sweetest fruits of following Christ. But it rarely comes through rushing, proving, or comparing. It comes through learning of Him. Listening to Him. Walking with Him.

Christ's peace is not just the absence of chaos. It is the presence of calm confidence that God is with you. That He knows your heart and honors your effort. It grows in quiet, steady places. In scripture study. In prayer. In honest trying.

One woman said she used to chase peace through perfect checklists. When she finally slowed down and just tried to be with Christ—reading one verse, offering one real prayer—peace found her instead.

You do not have to master everything today. Just take one step with Christ and let Him walk the rest with you.

Today, slow your pace. Take time to learn of Christ and listen for His words. Peace will follow.

What can you do today to better walk in the meekness of His Spirit?

January 15

> *"For behold, I am God; and I am a God of miracles; and I will show unto the world that I am the same yesterday, today, and forever; and I work not among the children of men save it be according to their faith."*
>
> 2 Nephi 27:23

Sometimes we believe God can work miracles, just not for us. We trust He parted the Red Sea and raised the dead, but we doubt He can heal our hearts or help us change. But He hasn't changed. And He is still a God of miracles.

A miracle isn't always a sudden, dramatic change. Often, it's quiet strength to keep going, courage to forgive, or hope that returns after a long night of worry. Christ performs miracles both boldly and gently.

One young man shared that he began each morning praying for "miracle eyes," a heart and vision attuned to recognize God's miracles throughout the day. His routine stayed the same, but his spirit changed. He began seeing grace where he once felt only frustration.

Miracles are not rare. Sometimes they are just quiet. Look for them. Believe in them. Expect them.

Today, pray with faith in the God of miracles. Ask to see His hand in something small and sacred.

What miracle are you hoping for? How can you show faith that God is already preparing it?

January 16

> *"Behold, I am Jesus Christ, whom the prophets testified shall come into the world."*
>
> *"And behold, I am the light and the life of the world; ..."*
>
> 3 Nephi 11:10-11

When life feels dark or uncertain, it's easy to look everywhere for light, except to the One who is the source of it. But Christ doesn't just offer light. He is the Light. And He is never out of reach.

Light changes everything. It reveals what's true. It brings warmth. It gives direction. When you begin your day, your goals, or your healing with Christ, you're stepping out of confusion and into clarity.

A mother once said that during one of the hardest years of her life, she made a quiet decision to begin every morning by speaking His name out loud. "Jesus Christ," she would say. That simple act didn't solve her problems, but it shifted her perspective. It reminded her who was with her.

When Christ is your Light, you're never truly in the dark.

Today, begin your day with Christ. Speak His name, read His words, or simply sit in stillness and feel His presence.

Where do you need more light in your life right now? How can you let Christ bring it in?

January 17

> *"We love him, because he first loved us."*
> 1 John 4:19

Before you ever turned your heart to Christ, He had already turned His toward you. His love came first. It always does.

That love isn't based on your record, your knowledge, or your strength. It's not something you earn. It's something you accept and allow to change you.

Think of a child learning to walk. The parent doesn't love them more when they get it right and less when they fall. The love is constant. Unshaken. That's how Christ loves you. He rejoices in your growth, but He never withdraws His love when you struggle.

One woman said she used to worry whether she loved Christ enough. But then she realized the real miracle was how completely He loved her, even in her weakness. That truth gave her the courage to keep going.

You don't begin with love for Him. You begin by letting His love reach you.

Today, instead of trying to prove your love for Christ, pause and receive His love for you. Let that be your starting place.

How might your choices today be different if you truly believe Christ loves you as you are?

January 18

> *"But behold, ye have both heard my voice, and seen me; and ye are my sheep, and ye are numbered among those whom the Father hath given me."*
>
> 3 Nephi 15:24

Learning to recognize the voice of the Lord is one of the most personal parts of discipleship. It doesn't always come through thunder or dreams. More often, it sounds like clarity in your thoughts, peace in your heart, or a truth you can't ignore.

Christ is the Good Shepherd. He knows your name. And He is always speaking—guiding, comforting, correcting, calling. The question is never whether He is speaking. The question is whether we are quiet enough to listen.

One brother said that when he finally turned off the noise—less scrolling, fewer distractions—he began to notice the Lord's voice in ways he hadn't before. "It wasn't that God started speaking," he said. "It was that I finally started listening."

You don't need to be perfect to hear Him. You just need to be still enough to notice.

Today, set aside a moment of stillness. Ask the Lord what He wants you to hear, and listen with real intent.

When have you clearly recognized the Lord's voice in your life? What helps you hear Him now?

January 19

> *"The Spirit itself beareth witness with our spirit, that we are the children of God:"*
> Romans 8:16

There is something powerful about being reminded who you really are. Not who the world says you should be, or who your fears tell you you're not, but who God declares you are.

You are His child. Not metaphorically. Literally. And that truth changes everything.

It means you are not forgotten. You are not unseen. You are not without help. Because children have access to their Father, and He is a perfect one—ever present, endlessly patient, eternally loving.

A returned missionary once shared how this verse carried him through a season of self-doubt. Each time he read it, he would pause and say aloud, "I am a child of God." Over time, that truth settled into his bones and softened how he saw himself.

You don't have to earn God's love or prove your worth. You just have to remember who you've always been.

Today, say it out loud: "I am a child of God." Let that identity shape how you show up in the world.

How would your choices, your thoughts, or your prayers change if you truly believed you were His?

January 20

> *"If any of you lack wisdom, let him ask of God, that giveth to all men liberally, and upbraideth not; and it shall be given him."*
>
> James 1:5

The ability to begin again doesn't just come from desire. It comes from direction. And God is ready to give it. Personally, clearly, and generously.

When Joseph Smith read this verse, it changed history. But the promise wasn't just for him. It's for you too. You can ask God for wisdom in your confusion, in your decision-making, in your heartache, and in your next steps.

Revelation is not reserved for prophets alone. It belongs to every child of God who asks with faith and listens with humility.

One woman kept a small notebook labeled "Questions for God." As she studied and prayed, she wrote her impressions in the notebook. Over time, the answers came—some slowly, some clearly—but always in the Lord's way and time.

Your questions are not a sign of weak faith. They're a sign that you believe God has answers.

Today, write down a question you have for the Lord. Take it to Him in prayer and watch for how He responds.

What wisdom do you need right now? Are you making space to hear His answer?

January 21

> *"... Let virtue garnish thy thoughts unceasingly; then shall thy confidence wax strong in the presence of God. ..."*
> Doctrine and Covenants 121:45

Confidence is a quiet strength that grows from within. It doesn't come from applause or success, but from a heart aligned with God. When your thoughts center on what is pure, and uplifting, something shifts. You begin to feel more at peace with who you are and who you are becoming.

Virtue isn't just about morality. It's about spiritual clarity. It's the kind of thinking that invites the Spirit and strengthens your identity as a disciple of Christ.

One woman began paying closer attention to her thoughts. She noticed what she focused on, what she consumed, and what she repeated to herself. As she adjusted those patterns, she found more confidence in prayer, more clarity in decisions, and more peace in her mind.

Spiritual confidence isn't loud. It's steady. And it grows with every thought that draws you closer to Christ.

Today, choose to notice your thoughts. Invite more virtue in and watch how it strengthens your confidence before God.

What thoughts are shaping your spiritual confidence? What could you change to draw closer to Christ?

January 22

> *"For the natural man is an enemy to God... unless he yields to the enticings of the Holy Spirit..."*
>
> Mosiah 3:19

Becoming more like Christ isn't about pretending you don't struggle. It's about yielding and choosing to let the Spirit lead when your natural instincts want to react, retreat, or resist.

The "natural man" shows up in impatience, comparison, selfishness, and fear. But the Spirit speaks with gentleness. It nudges you to try again, to be softer, to listen longer, to forgive faster.

One brother shared that he started noticing a pattern: when he paused to pray before reacting, the Spirit always offered a better way. It didn't erase his emotions, but it gave him perspective. He said, "Yielding didn't make me weaker. It made me freer."

Spiritual strength comes when you choose Christ over impulse, and grace over pride.

Today, when a natural reaction rises up, pause. Yield to the Spirit and watch how Christ softens your heart.

What part of your natural self could you surrender more fully to the Savior today?

January 23

> "Wherefore, ye must press forward with a steadfastness in Christ, having a perfect brightness of hope, and a love of God and of all men..."
>
> 2 Nephi 31:20

Some days, pressing forward feels like climbing a mountain. Other days, it feels like barely crawling. But the invitation is the same: keep going with Christ.

Steadfastness doesn't mean you never feel weary. It means you stay committed, even when the path is hard. It means you lean on Christ, not your own strength. And it means you let hope light the way, even when you can't see the finish line.

A young mother once said she held onto this verse when life felt overwhelming. Every day she prayed for just enough hope to take the next step. And every day, she found it. Not all at once, but enough. Enough to keep pressing forward.

Hope in Christ is not vague or wishful. It is real and steady. It's the kind of hope that moves you forward when nothing else can.

Today, press forward in whatever way you can. Trust that Christ is walking with you and that hope is never wasted.

Where do you need more hope right now? How can Christ help you hold on to it?

January 24

> *"... And my grace is sufficient for all men that humble themselves before me; ..."*
>
> Ether 12:27

Grace isn't something you earn once you've done enough. It's the strength you receive because Christ has already done everything. It meets you where you are and helps you become what you could never be on your own.

We're often taught to push through, to be strong, to try harder. But grace teaches us to kneel first. To admit we can't do it alone. That kind of humility isn't weakness. It is power, because it opens the door for Christ to step in.

One man said he used to think grace was just for big, dramatic moments. But he began to pray for it in small things, such as patience in traffic or peace in a tense conversation. The more he asked, the more he received. And he realized that grace wasn't rare. It was constant.

Grace changes effort into progress and weakness into strength. It is always enough.

Today, ask for grace. Not just to endure, but to grow. Then notice the ways Christ helps you along the way.

What's one area of your life that needs less self-pressure and more of Christ's grace?

January 25

> *"And now, behold, I say unto you, that the thing which will be of the most worth unto you will be to declare repentance unto this people, that you may bring souls unto me, that you may rest with them in the kingdom of my Father. Amen."*
>
> Doctrine and Covenants 15:6

Repentance is often misunderstood. It's not just a way to fix failures. It's the path that keeps us close to Christ. It's a gift, not a punishment. A cleansing, not a condemnation.

To repent is to turn. To return. To realign your heart with heaven. It's what allows every fresh start possible. Not because you're suddenly flawless, but because you're willing to be changed.

One young woman once dreaded repentance, thinking it meant she had failed. But as she studied the Savior's words, she began to see it as love. "Repentance didn't mean I was unworthy," she said. "It meant Christ still believed in me enough to help me grow."

With Christ, repentance isn't something to fear. It's something to trust.

Today, take one honest look inward. Ask the Lord what He would have you change and let Him help you.

How can you shift your view of repentance to see it as a hopeful return rather than a painful retreat?

January 26

> *"The joy we feel has little to do with the circumstances of our lives and everything to do with the focus of our lives."*
> President Russell M. Nelson

Joy isn't just an end goal in the gospel. It is a vital part of the journey. You were created to feel it. Not just someday, but now. And not just when life is perfect, but even in the middle of the mess.

When your life begins with Christ, joy becomes more than fleeting happiness. It becomes a quiet assurance that God is with you. A feeling that lingers even when the day is hard. A strength that bubbles up from truth, not circumstances.

One sister said she started looking for "joy snapshots" each day. These were simple moments that made her smile or feel God's love. A text from a friend. A scripture that spoke to her. A quiet moment of peace. She said, "The more I looked for joy, the more I realized it had been there all along."

Christ doesn't just offer joy. He is joy. And He is with you.

Today, look for a small moment of joy. Let it remind you that you were created for this.

What brings you true, lasting joy? How can you invite more of it into your life with Christ?

January 27

> *"Come unto me, all ye that labour and are heavy laden, and I will give you rest."*
> Matthew 11:28

There's a kind of tired that sleep doesn't fix. It's the weariness that settles into the soul. It comes from carrying burdens you were never meant to carry alone.

Christ's invitation to "come unto me" isn't just for those who have it all together. It's for the overwhelmed, the anxious, the stretched thin. It's for anyone trying to do their best but feeling like it's not enough.

One woman shared that during a hard season, she imagined placing her burdens in the Savior's hands during prayer. At first, it felt symbolic. But over time, it became real. Her problems didn't vanish, but her strength increased. And her rest deepened.

Rest is not always an escape. Sometimes it's the peace you feel in the middle of the storm because you know Christ is with you.

Today, bring one burden to Christ in sincere prayer. Let Him carry what you no longer can.

What weight have you been holding alone that Christ is willing to help you lift?

January 28

> *"... Sanctify yourselves: for to morrow the Lord will do wonders among you."*
>
> Joshua 3:5

God's miracles are often preceded by preparation. Not because He needs it, but because we do. A prepared heart is more able to recognize, receive, and rejoice in what the Lord is doing.

To sanctify yourself doesn't mean to be spotless. It means to set yourself apart for something sacred. It means clearing out distractions, recommitting to truth, and creating space for the Spirit to dwell.

One young man turned off his music during his commute and prayed instead. The change was minor, but the effect was deep. "I started to notice spiritual impressions that had always been there," he said. "I had just been too distracted to hear them."

You don't need to do something huge to prepare for God's wonders. You just need to offer your heart.

Today, do one thing to set yourself apart spiritually. Watch how even small sanctifying acts can open the way for God to work.

What could you remove or rearrange in your life to create more space for the Spirit to speak and for Christ to lead?

January 29

> *"... I will go before your face. I will be on your right hand and on your left... and mine angels round about you, to bear you up."*
> Doctrine and Covenants 84:88

There is great comfort in knowing you never walk alone. Christ doesn't just send help, He *is* the help. He goes before you, beside you, and around you. His presence is constant, even when your awareness isn't.

We often face unknowns with fear. But what if we faced them with faith in who walks ahead? What if the next step wasn't about courage, but about trust?

A young woman preparing for a major life change said this verse became her anchor. "I couldn't see how everything would work out," she said. "But I believed Christ *could* work it out. And that was enough to move forward."

Christ is not a distant guide. He is an ever-present companion. And when you begin with Him, you are never without strength.

Today, remember who goes before you. Walk forward with trust, even if the path ahead isn't clear yet.

Where in your life do you need to trust that Christ is already ahead of you, preparing the way?

January 30

> *"Therefore, if ye have desires to serve God ye are called to the work;"*
>
> Doctrine and Covenants 4:3

You don't have to be perfect to have purpose. In the Lord's eyes, desire matters. A willing heart is often the beginning of a powerful journey.

Sometimes we wait to feel more qualified before we act. We hesitate to speak up, to serve, to reach out, thinking we don't know enough or haven't done enough. But the Lord calls those who desire to serve, not just those who already seem ready.

One man said that when he was asked to serve in a calling that felt overwhelming, he almost said no. But then he remembered the verse in the Doctrine and Covenants (above). "I realized the Lord wasn't asking for expertise," he said. "He was asking for effort. I could give that."

The Lord magnifies what we offer, however small it seems. He works with desire and grows it into something meaningful.

Today, offer your heart to the Lord's work, whatever that may look like for you right now. He will meet you where you are.

Where is the Lord inviting you to serve, and how can you show willingness even before you feel ready?

January 31

> *"Therefore let your light so shine before this people, that they may see your good works and glorify your Father who is in heaven."*
>
> 3 Nephi 12:16

Your light doesn't need to be loud to be real. It doesn't have to impress anyone. It only needs to reflect Christ.

Beginning with Him means letting His love, truth, and kindness flow through you into the lives of others. You may not always feel like you're making a difference, but when you live with Him at the center, your light makes more impact than you realize.

One teacher shared that she used to feel unnoticed in her small acts of service. Then one day, a student told her, "You make me feel safe." That quiet comment changed everything. Her light had been shining all along. She just hadn't seen it.

Christ never asked us to create our own light. He only asked us to let His shine through.

Today, live in a way that reflects Christ's goodness. Let your light shine gently but clearly.

What is one Christlike quality you can share more of with those around you today?

February

Love like Christ loves by being kind, offering grace, and ministering with a compassionate heart.

February 1

> *"But charity is the pure love of Christ, and it endureth forever; and whoso is found possessed of it at the last day, it shall be well with him."*
> Moroni 7:47

CHARITY IS NOT JUST kindness or affection. It is the divine love that sees past flaws, forgives quickly, and gives freely. It is the kind of love Christ lived every moment of His life.

Loving like Christ begins in the heart, not in the headlines. It shows up in everyday choices. In how you listen, how you speak, how you serve, and how you see others. Charity is not reserved for the extraordinary. It is practiced in the ordinary.

One woman shared how she began praying each morning for charity, specifically asking to see others the way Christ sees them. She said the change didn't come all at once, but slowly her reactions softened. Her judgments quieted. Her compassion grew.

Christlike love isn't always natural, but it is always possible through Him.

Today, pray for the gift of charity. Ask Christ to help you see someone through His eyes.

> **Where in your life can you show more of the pure love of Christ? What would that look like in action?**

February 2

> *"By this shall all men know that ye are my disciples, if ye have love one to another."*
> John 13:35

Jesus didn't say the world would recognize His disciples by their titles, knowledge, or achievements. He said they would know us by our love.

That kind of love isn't passive. It reaches. It sees. It acts. It ministers in the quiet moments, in the interruptions, and in the inconvenience. Christlike love goes beyond courtesy. It enters into people's lives with compassion and a willingness to stay.

One man shared that after the profound loss of his wife, it wasn't the words people said that helped the most. It was the way they showed up. A text. A meal. A hug. Their love didn't fix the pain, but it helped him feel less alone.

Love is the mark of discipleship. When we love like Christ, people feel it. And more importantly, they feel Him.

Today, ask the Lord who needs your love and attention. Then reach out in a small but meaningful way.

What would it look like to be known as a disciple of Christ by how you love?

February 3

> *"And behold, I tell you these things that ye may learn wisdom; that ye may learn that when ye are in the service of your fellow beings ye are only in the service of your God."*
>
> Mosiah 2:17

Loving like Christ often looks like serving without spotlight. It's the small and simple things. The lifted load, the answered text, the quiet help that no one else sees.

Ministering doesn't require a formal assignment. It requires a willing heart. When you serve others with love, you are standing in Christ's place. And that changes ordinary efforts into sacred work.

One young adult woman said she started asking each morning, "Who needs something today?" Sometimes the answer came in a name. Other times, in a feeling. But as she followed those impressions, her days felt fuller. She said, "Loving people helped me feel closer to Jesus."

Christlike service blesses both the giver and the receiver. It binds hearts. It builds faith. It brings heaven a little closer.

Today, serve someone without being asked. Let your love speak through your actions.

How can you make ministering a natural part of your life rather than just an assignment?

February 4

> *"Blessed are the merciful: for they shall obtain mercy."*
>
> Matthew 5:7

Mercy is love in motion. It steps in with compassion when judgment would be easier. It chooses to see a person, not just a problem. When we show mercy, we reflect the Savior, who has shown it to us more times than we can count.

To love like Christ means to give others room to grow. To offer the kind of grace we hope to receive. That doesn't mean excusing harm or ignoring truth. It means letting the Atonement cover more than just our own mistakes. It means believing that change is possible for everyone.

One man said he used to struggle with resentment until he prayed to see someone through Christ's eyes. The answer didn't come instantly. But over time, the bitterness faded. What remained was empathy. And peace.

When we extend mercy, we invite the Spirit to soften hearts. Sometimes, the heart that changes first is our own.

Today, choose mercy. Let it shape how you think, speak, and respond.

Is there someone you could see with more compassion if you asked Christ to help you?

February 5

> *"A new commandment I give unto you, That ye love one another; as I have loved you, that ye also love one another."*
>
> John 13:34

Christ's love is the pattern. It is patient, forgiving, and full of grace. It lifts instead of criticizes. It listens instead of reacts. And it stays, even when things get uncomfortable or hard.

To love like Christ is to love with commitment. It is not based on convenience or agreement. It's a choice made again and again. To see others not just for who they are today, but for who they can become.

A friend of mine said she began trying to ask herself a single question when someone frustrated her. "How would Christ love them right now?" That question softened her tone. It opened her heart. It reminded her that love isn't just a feeling. It's a way of seeing.

The Savior's love changes people. And it begins with how we choose to love each other.

Today, love someone more intentionally. Let Christ guide your words and your heart.

What might shift in your relationships if you tried to love others the way Christ loves you?

February 6

> *"... Lift up the hands which hang down, and strengthen the feeble knees."*
> Doctrine and Covenants 81:5

Loving like Christ often means noticing. It means seeing what others overlook and being willing to act. Sometimes the miracle someone needs is simply to not feel invisible.

Christ was always aware of those around Him. The woman who touched His robe. The man by the pool. The overlooked, the weary, the forgotten. He noticed them, and He responded.

One sister said she made it a goal to truly see people each day. Not just pass them, but notice them. A tired cashier. A quiet neighbor. A struggling child. As she looked closer, she found more chances to lift, listen, and love.

We do not need to fix everything. But we can offer presence. We can offer encouragement. We can lift the hands that hang down, one small gesture at a time.

Today, look for someone who might need lifting. Be the answer to a prayer they haven't yet spoken.

What helps you notice people the way Christ would? How can you act on that today?

February 7

> *"This is my commandment, That ye love one another, as I have loved you."*
>
> John 15:12

Christ's love was not selective. He loved the sinners and the seekers, the doubters and the devoted. He loved with open arms and open hands, without waiting for others to be worthy of it.

To love like Christ is to reach beyond comfort. It is to sit with someone in their sorrow, to forgive when it is undeserved, to extend kindness when none is expected. This kind of love doesn't always feel convenient. But it always invites the Spirit.

One man said he once held a grudge for months, until he read this verse and felt the Spirit whisper, "Let Me love them through you." That changed everything. He realized that he didn't have to generate the love on his own. He just needed to open his heart and let Christ fill it.

The love of Christ is not something we store. It is something we share.

Today, ask Christ to love someone through you. Watch how that changes your heart and theirs.

What would it look like to let Christ's love flow through you toward someone you find hard to love?

February 8

> *"Bear ye one another's burdens, and so fulfil the law of Christ."*
>
> Galatians 6:2

Loving like Christ means shouldering some of the weight that others are carrying. Not because we can fix it, but because no one should have to carry it alone.

Christ bore the ultimate burden. He descended below all things so that He could lift us in all things. When we bear each other's burdens, we walk a little more like Him. We remind others that they are not forgotten, and we remind ourselves of what it means to be His.

One woman said she never forgot the day someone sat with her in silence after a heartbreak. No advice. No distractions. Just presence. "That was the day I learned what ministering meant," she said. "It meant not letting someone feel alone."

Sometimes the best kind of help isn't what we say, but how we stay.

Today, find a way to share someone's burden. Let them feel the strength of Christ through you.

Who in your life might be carrying something heavy? How can you help lift it today?

February 9

> *"Love is the measure of our faith, the inspiration for our obedience, and the true altitude of our discipleship."*
> Elder Dieter F. Uchtdorf

Love is not just a feeling. It is a divine force that shapes our actions and defines our discipleship. When we love as Christ loves, our faith deepens, our obedience becomes joyful, and our lives align more closely with His teachings.

One young woman shared that she began to see a change in her daily interactions when she consciously chose to act with love. Simple acts like listening attentively, offering a kind word, or extending a helping hand became opportunities to express her faith. She realized that these small choices, rooted in love, brought her closer to Christ and strengthened her relationships.

Christlike love transforms ordinary moments into sacred experiences. It invites the Spirit, fosters unity, and reflects the Savior's light to those around us.

Today, let love guide your actions. Seek opportunities to serve, uplift, and connect with others in meaningful ways.

How can you make love the foundation of your discipleship today?

February 10

> *"As I have loved you, love one another. This new commandment: Love one another ..."*
> Love One Another, Hymn No. 308

To love like Christ is to meet people where they are. It is to see them through eyes of compassion, not comparison. Christ never waited for people to have it all together. He loved them in their becoming.

That kind of love doesn't always come easily. It requires patience, humility, and a willingness to let go of expectations. But when we choose to love with grace, we make space for others to grow and for the Spirit to work.

One man shared that he used to get frustrated when people didn't meet his standards. But then he felt prompted to pray, not that others would change, but that *he* would. The more he prayed, the more his heart softened. Love became less about others meeting his expectations and more about him reflecting the Savior.

Loving like Christ means loving people while they are still growing. Just as He loves us.

Today, give someone the gift of grace. Love them as they are, not as you wish they were.

What expectations could you release in order to love someone more like Christ would?

February 11

> *"My little children, let us not love in word,
> neither in tongue; but in deed and in truth."*
> 1 John 3:18

Love is more than kind thoughts and warm feelings. It becomes real when it moves into action. Christ didn't just speak love. He lived it. He healed, fed, forgave, and lifted. His love was visible.

To love like Him is to act on the promptings we feel. It might mean making the call, offering the help, or showing up when it would be easier not to. Loving in deed means we don't just feel compassion. We do something about it.

One brother shared that he started setting a reminder each day to act on one small prompting of love. Sometimes it led to a message, sometimes a visit, sometimes a quiet prayer for someone else. "It changed how I lived," he said. "I stopped waiting for big moments and started creating small ones."

Love in action becomes a testimony of who we follow.

Today, act on one feeling of love you've been holding in your heart. Let it become something visible.

What is one small action you can take today to show real love in Christ's name?

February 12

> *"... for the Lord seeth not as man seeth; for man looketh on the outward appearance, but the Lord looketh on the heart."*
>
> 1 Samuel 16:7

One of the most Christlike ways we can love is by looking deeper. The Savior sees more than what others show. He understands motives, wounds, and efforts that are often hidden from view.

To love like Him is to slow down before judging. It is to ask for spiritual eyes. To see hearts instead of labels, potential instead of problems. This kind of love transforms how we relate to family, friends, and even strangers.

One woman said she was struggling with a difficult coworker until she prayed to see him the way God did. The next day, her view shifted. She noticed signs of stress and isolation. Compassion replaced irritation. Nothing about him changed, but everything about her response did.

Christlike love looks past appearances. It reaches for the heart.

Today, ask the Lord to help you see someone differently. Look beyond the surface and let love lead.

Who in your life might need to be seen through spiritual eyes instead of worldly ones?

February 13

> *"May we show our gratitude and love for God by ministering with love to our eternal sisters and brothers."*
>
> Sister Jean B. Bingham

Loving like Christ does not require grand gestures. It often looks like small, Spirit-led actions done with sincere care. A note. A kind word. A short prayer. These are the tools of true discipleship.

When we minister with love, we become instruments in the Lord's hands. Our simple acts become sacred as the Spirit magnifies them. What may seem small to us can be exactly what someone else needs.

One man said he received a short text from a friend during a hard week. Just a few words, but they felt like a lifeline. "He didn't even know what I was going through," the man said. "But the Lord did."

Love doesn't have to be loud to be life-changing.

Today, do one small thing with love and intention. Let the Spirit guide you to someone who needs it.

What simple act of love can you offer today that might lift someone more than you know?

February 14

> *"Charity never faileth ..."*
> 1 Corinthians 13:8

The world often celebrates love today with cards, flowers, and chocolates. These gestures are sweet, but the love Christ invites us to give and receive is far deeper and more lasting. It doesn't fade with time or depend on perfection. It is patient. It is selfless. It endures.

Charity—the pure love of Christ—is the kind of love that lifts when romance fades, that comforts in grief, and that remains when things are hard. It's the love that forgives, that stays, that heals. It's the love that Christ offers us every day.

One couple shared that after decades of marriage, what kept them strong wasn't grand romantic gestures. It was daily kindness. Shared prayers. Service during illness. Gentle words in tense moments. "That's when we felt closest to the Savior," they said, "when we loved each other the way He loves us."

On this day, when love is celebrated, let us remember the greatest love of all. The love of Christ. And let it shape how we love each other.

Today, express Christlike love to someone in a thoughtful way. Let them feel seen, valued, and cherished.

How can you deepen your love for others by making it more like His?

February 15

> "He that is faithful and endureth shall overcome the world."
> Doctrine and Covenants 63:47

Loving like Christ means choosing love even when it's not easy. It means enduring in relationships that challenge us, showing grace when it's hard to give, and staying kind when others are not. True love is not tested in ease, but in endurance.

Enduring love is steady. It forgives more than once. It listens more than it speaks. It doesn't withdraw when things get difficult. Christ's love never gives up on us. And when we love like Him, we learn to offer that same patience to others.

One mother said that during a tough season with her teenager, she clung to prayer and quiet service. "I chose to stay soft," she said. "Not because it was easy, but because I wanted my child to feel Christ's love through me."

Love that lasts comes from the Savior. He strengthens our hearts when they are weary and helps us love longer than we thought we could.

Today, practice enduring love. Stay gentle, patient, or present even when it's hard.

What helps you keep loving when it would be easier to stop? How can Christ sustain you in that effort?

February 16

> *"We are the Lord's hands here upon the earth, with the mandate to serve and to lift His children."*
>
> President Thomas S. Monson

To love like Christ is to serve like Christ. Not out of obligation, but out of desire. Not for praise, but for love. His service was always personal, always timely, and always full of compassion.

When we step into someone's life with the intent to lift, we fulfill more than a need. We reflect the Savior. Our hands, our words, and our willingness become the means through which He reaches His children.

One woman said she decided to treat every day as a chance to be someone's miracle. Whether through a smile, a message, or a quiet act of kindness, she asked, "Lord, who needs You today through me?" The answers came. So did the joy.

Love that serves becomes sacred. And service done with love brings us closer to Christ.

Today, be the Lord's hands. Ask who needs lifting and look for ways to act on the answer.

What would it look like to treat each day as a chance to serve the Lord by serving others?

February 17

> *"And they had all things common among them; therefore there were not rich and poor, bond and free, but they were all made free, and partakers of the heavenly gift."*
>
> 4 Nephi 1:3

When love fills a community, division fades. Needs are seen. People are equal not in status, but in worth. That's the vision Christ gave us. Not a perfect society, but a loving one.

To love like Christ is to recognize that we are all brothers and sisters. It's to see past surface differences and focus on shared divinity. It's to care when someone lacks, to rejoice when someone rises, and to carry each other through.

One man said he felt the purest sense of belonging not during a big Church event, but when a neighbor brought over a meal after surgery. "It wasn't just the food," he said. "It was the feeling that I mattered."

Christlike love creates Zion wherever it is practiced. It turns neighbors into family.

Today, notice someone who might be feeling left out or left behind. Reach out and remind them they belong.

What can you do to help build a spirit of unity and love in your home, ward, or community?

February 18

> *"Kindness is the essence of a celestial life. Kindness is how a Christlike person treats others."*
>
> Elder Joseph B. Wirthlin

Kindness may seem simple, but it holds the power to soften hearts, heal wounds, and open doors to the Spirit. It is love in its most approachable form. Quiet, consistent, and sincere.

Christ's kindness was never rushed or forced. It met people in their need, without judgment. To follow Him is to treat others with that same gentle strength. Kindness doesn't require agreement or deep connection. It simply requires love.

One teenager said that during a lonely year at school, one classmate's daily smile changed everything. "It reminded me I wasn't invisible," she said. "That kindness pulled me through."

You never know what someone is carrying. But you can always offer something kind.

Today, choose deliberate kindness. Look for one way to brighten someone's path.

How can you develop a habit of kindness that reflects the love of Christ?

February 19

> *"... I say unto you, be one; and if ye are not one ye are not mine."*
> Doctrine and Covenants 38:27

Unity is more than agreement. It is the decision to value connection over contention and charity over criticism. To love like Christ is to build bridges where there could be walls and to seek peace where there could be pride.

The Savior prayed we would be one. Not because we are all the same, but because we are all His. Differences don't have to divide us when love leads us.

One Relief Society sister said she started praying not to change others' opinions, but to understand their hearts. That prayer changed her. She began to see people not as problems to fix, but as souls to love.

Christlike love fosters unity. It makes room for growth, for grace, and for the Spirit to work.

Today, look for a chance to build unity. Let love guide how you interact, even with those who see things differently.

What would change in your relationships if you chose a connection over being right?

February 20

> *"Wherefore, be faithful; stand in the office which I have appointed unto you; succor the weak, lift up the hands which hang down, and strengthen the feeble knees."*
> Doctrine and Covenants 81:5

Christlike love moves us to action. It doesn't wait for convenience. It sees a need and responds with compassion, even when it's quiet or unnoticed.

To love like Christ is to be willing to strengthen others, even when you feel weak yourself. It's offering encouragement when you're not sure what to say. It's standing with someone, simply so they don't have to stand alone.

One bishop shared that during a particularly heavy week, a child in the ward drew him a picture and handed it to him after sacrament meeting. "You look tired," she said. "I thought this would help." It did. A small act of love became a sustaining gift.

Your offering doesn't need to be big. It just needs to be real.

Today, lift someone who feels low. Offer what you can, and let Christ magnify it.

What small gesture of love or strength can you give to someone who may need it today?

February 21

> "... And except they should have charity they were nothing. ..."
>
> 2 Nephi 26:30

Charity is not just a spiritual gift. It's the foundation of everything that lasts. Without charity, even our best efforts can fall flat.

To love like Christ is to let charity guide not only what you do, but *how* you do it. It's the tone in your voice, the patience in your response, and the kindness in your correction. Charity transforms our discipleship from duty into devotion.

One mission leader said that when he began focusing more on loving his missionaries than fixing their problems, everything shifted. At first, he felt pressure to correct, instruct, and manage every challenge. But over time, he realized what they needed most wasn't constant correction. It was connection. "They didn't just improve," he said. "They started to flourish. Love helped them grow." As he spent more time listening, encouraging, and praying with them, he saw their confidence rise and their faith deepen.

Love invites growth. It creates safety. It points us back to Christ.

Today, ask yourself if charity is at the root of your actions. Let it shape how you serve, speak, and lead.

How would your relationships change if charity became your daily motive?

February 22

> *"Let us all press on in the work of the Lord."*
> Let Us All Press On, Hymn no. 243

Loving like Christ isn't a one-time effort. It's a daily decision. It's choosing to keep showing up, even when it's hard. It's pressing forward in love when you're tired, when you've been hurt, or when it feels like no one notices.

Christ's ministry was filled with moments that demanded endurance. He experienced long days, little rest, and much rejection. But He never stopped loving. He pressed on because love was His mission.

One Relief Society president said she once felt overwhelmed by the needs in her ward. But instead of stepping back, she stepped into prayer. "I realized I wasn't expected to do everything," she said, "just to love faithfully, one person at a time." That shift gave her strength.

Love that endures is powerful. It keeps us moving forward, hand in hand with Christ.

Today, keep pressing forward in love. Even small acts count when done with Christ in your heart.

Where do you need endurance in your efforts to love and serve others? How can Christ sustain you in that?

February 23

"We love him, because he first loved us."
1 John 4:19

All our efforts to love others begin with this simple truth: Christ loved us first. Before we repented, before we prayed, before we even knew His name, He loved us. That love is what changes us. It's what enables us to love more deeply, more patiently, and more freely.

When we struggle to love someone who's difficult, or to forgive someone who's hurt us, remembering His love brings clarity. He didn't wait for us to deserve His grace. He gave it anyway. And He invites us to do the same.

One woman said she started keeping a gratitude journal, not just for blessings, but for moments she felt the love of God. "When I realized how often He loved me through others," she said, "I wanted to be that for someone else."

The more we recognize Christ's love, the more we're able to share it.

Today, reflect on how Christ has shown His love for you. Let that love inspire you to reach out to someone else.

What does it mean to you that Christ loved you first? How can you reflect that love today?

February 24

> *"Rather than being judgmental and critical of each other, may we have the pure love of Christ for our fellow travelers in this journey through life."*
>
> President Thomas S. Monson

Judgment is easy. It requires little effort and little understanding. Love, on the other hand, asks for more. It asks us to listen, to withhold assumptions, and to remember that we never see the full story.

Christ never rushed to judge. He reached, taught, lifted, and healed. He knew hearts, and He still chose compassion. To love like Him is to trade criticism for curiosity, to replace assumptions with grace.

One young adult said she used to feel distant from someone in her ward until she made a goal to ask about their life instead of making guesses. That one conversation changed everything. "I realized I had misunderstood them for years," she said. "And I nearly missed the chance to love them."

Love opens doors that judgment keeps closed. And it transforms both the giver and the receiver.

Today, choose love over judgment. Give someone the benefit of the doubt and seek to understand.

Where in your life might love soften a harsh assumption or help mend a strained relationship?

February 25

> *"By this shall all men know that ye are my disciples, if ye have love one to another."*
> John 13:35

Love is the clearest mark of discipleship. It's not how much we know, how long we've served, or how often we speak in church. It's how we treat each other, especially when it's hard.

To love like Christ is to let love be the message, not just the motive. It shows in how we welcome others, how we respond to failure, and how we speak when no one else is listening. Love, more than anything, reveals who we follow.

One stake leader said that after a challenging meeting, she felt impressed not to argue a point, but to quietly affirm someone who had felt unheard. "I realized my role wasn't to win," she said. "It was to represent Christ." That moment built trust and softened hearts.

Our discipleship is most visible in our relationships. The more we reflect Christ's love, the more others will recognize Him in us.

Today, reflect on how your love for others testifies of Christ. Let it show in word and action.

If someone watched how you treat others, what would it tell them about your discipleship?

February 26

> *"Often small acts of service are all that is required to lift and bless another."*
> President Thomas S. Monson

The Savior's love often came through quiet moments. A touch, a look, a word. He didn't need a crowd to make a difference, just a heart willing to reach out.

Sometimes we underestimate what small acts can do. But in the hands of the Lord, they become sacred. A warm meal. A kind note. A few minutes to listen. These simple things carry His love into places we may never see.

One woman said she decided to keep a note card and pen in her bag. When prompted, she'd write a quick message to someone on her mind. "It only took a moment," she said, "but more than once, the person told me it came right when they needed it."

Love doesn't have to be dramatic to be divine. It just needs to be real.

Today, look for a small way to show someone they matter. Trust that it will reach further than you know.

What small act of love could you do today that might feel big to someone else?

February 27

> *"But charity is the pure love of Christ, and it endureth forever; ..."*
>
> Moroni 7:47

Charity doesn't just endure, it transforms. It softens hearts, deepens relationships, and builds a foundation that time and trials cannot shake. When we love with charity, we reflect the eternal love of the Savior.

This kind of love takes effort. It means forgiving even when it still hurts. It means serving when no one sees. It means choosing to believe the best in others, even when it would be easier not to. Charity isn't always comfortable. But it is always powerful.

One sister shared how her ministering sister checked in every month without fail, even when she didn't respond. "She didn't need anything from me," she said. "She just kept loving me. And eventually, I let her in." That patient, persistent love opened the door to healing. What touched her most wasn't the words or the timing, it was the consistency that made her feel remembered and worth reaching for.

Love that endures becomes love that heals.

Today, choose to love with charity. Let your care go deeper than convenience.

What would it look like to love someone with the same enduring grace Christ has shown you?

February 28

> *"... when ye are in the service of your fellow beings ye are only in the service of your God."*
> Mosiah 2:17

Service is not just something we give. It's something we become. When we serve with love, our hearts begin to mirror the Savior's. We start to see others the way He sees them, and we start to feel a deeper sense of purpose in our daily lives.

Christ didn't separate service from ministry or love from action. He combined them. Whether healing the sick or washing feet, He taught that the most powerful service often comes in the most humble ways.

One young woman said she started volunteering to deliver meals to an elderly neighbor. What began as a simple act turned into a friendship that blessed them both. "I thought I was helping her," she said, "but the truth is, she helped me become more like Christ."

Service given in love blesses everyone it touches.

Today, offer a simple act of service with a heart full of love. Let it be more than a task. Let it be ministry.

How can you make your everyday service more intentional and more Christlike?

February 29

> *"In family relationships, love is really spelled t-i-m-e, time."*
> Elder Dieter F. Uchtdorf

A leap day is a gift, an extra 24 hours we don't usually expect. What if we treated today not just as more time, but as more opportunity? More time to love, to minister, to become.

Christ never wasted time. His days were full of teaching, healing, and reaching. But they were also full of stillness, solitude, and prayer. He used His time to connect with others and to align with His Father.

One woman said that on leap day, she made a tradition of doing one act of pure, quiet love. Something outside her normal rhythm. One year it was writing letters of gratitude. Another year it was spending the day with someone who had no family nearby. "It became a sacred kind of day," she said. "A reminder that time, when given to God, becomes holy."

An extra day can become an eternal moment when it's filled with love.

Today, use your extra day for something meaningful. Let it reflect the Savior's love.

If today were a bonus gift of time from the Lord, how would you spend it in His service?

March

Follow Christ each day with faith, love, and steady steps of obedience.

March 1

"... come, follow me."

Luke 18:22

THE INVITATION IS SIMPLE. And personal. Christ doesn't just call crowds, He calls individuals. He looks into the heart and says, "Come." Not when you're ready. Not once you're perfect. But now.

To follow Him is to walk with Him. Step by step. Day by day. It means letting Him guide your choices, shape your thoughts, and teach your soul. It's not about keeping pace perfectly. It's about not turning back.

One young man said he used to think discipleship meant grand sacrifices. But as he began praying each morning, "What would Thou have me do today?" he discovered that following Christ often meant small, faithful choices. "It's not just a path," he said. "It's a relationship."

Discipleship is not a title. It's a way of life.

Today, ask the Lord how you can follow Him more intentionally. Then take one step, however small, in that direction.

What does it look like for you to follow Christ in your daily life, not just in belief, but in practice?

March 2

> *"With the gift of God's grace, the path of discipleship does not lead backward; it leads upward."*
>
> Elder Dieter F. Uchtdorf

Following Christ isn't about returning to where you once were. It's about rising, even slowly, to where He is. Discipleship means progress, however imperfect, however gradual. Through grace, every sincere effort lifts you higher.

Sometimes we confuse discipleship with spiritual perfection. But Christ isn't asking us to be flawless. He's asking us to be faithful. That means showing up when it's hard, forgiving ourselves when we fall short, and choosing Him again each day.

One woman said she used to feel discouraged when her scripture study wasn't deep or her prayers felt distracted. But over time, she realized the Lord honored her effort. "He didn't need it to be perfect," she said. "He just wanted it to be real."

The path of discipleship is not flat, it's upward. And grace is what helps us climb.

Today, take one upward step in your discipleship. Let grace guide you forward.

Where in your life do you feel Christ gently inviting you upward?

March 3

> *"... Yea, we believe all the words which thou hast spoken unto us; and also, we know of their surety and truth, because of the Spirit of the Lord Omnipotent, which has wrought a mighty change in us, or in our hearts ..."*
>
> Mosiah 5:2

Discipleship is born not just from hearing truth, but from feeling it. It's one thing to know the gospel in your mind. It's another to let it change your heart. The Spirit is what bridges that gap.

Following Christ means letting His words sink deeper than the surface. It means responding with conviction, not just curiosity. The people of King Benjamin didn't just listen, they believed. And then they acted. Their discipleship began with a spiritual witness and grew from there.

One man said that after a long season of spiritual complacency, he prayed to feel the truth again. "The change didn't come overnight," he said. "But slowly, the Spirit returned. And with it came the desire to truly follow."

The Spirit confirms the truth. And once truth is felt, it invites a life of discipleship.

Today, ask the Spirit to reaffirm what you already know is true. Let that witness inspire your next step.

What has the Spirit taught you recently that you're being invited to live more fully?

March 4

> *"... wherefore, follow me, and do the things which ye have seen me do."*
> 2 Nephi 31:12

To follow Christ is to pattern your life after His. Not just in the big, defining moments, but in the everyday ones. In the way you speak. The way you treat others. The way you respond to disappointment or offer grace in frustration.

Christ's life was filled with quiet obedience. He taught truth, but He also lived it. He didn't just preach love, He practiced it. He didn't just promise peace, He brought it.

One teacher said she began writing the question "What would Jesus do here?" at the top of her lesson plans each week. It wasn't about perfection. It was about intentionality. "It helped me teach with more compassion," she said. "It helped me lead more like Him."

Discipleship is more than belief. It's imitation. And the more you walk His path, the more your life begins to look like His.

Today, choose one way to model your actions more closely after Christ. Let Him shape your example.

What's one part of your life that could reflect Christ more clearly this week?

March 5

"May we be convinced that Jesus is the Christ, choose to follow Him, be changed for Him, captained by Him, consumed in Him, and born again I pray in the name of Jesus Christ, amen."

President Ezra Taft Benson

Following Christ is not just a direction, it's a transformation. You cannot walk His path and remain the same. The journey shapes you. It stretches your faith, refines your heart, and reveals who you really are.

Sometimes that change is subtle. It comes in softened words or gentler thoughts. Other times, it's dramatic. A shift in priorities, a surrender of pride, a renewed sense of purpose. But in every case, Christ leads us to become more than we were.

One convert said she was surprised by how natural the changes felt. "I didn't feel forced," she said. "I just felt drawn, to light, to peace, to Him. And little by little, I changed."

Discipleship doesn't demand instant transformation. It invites daily conversion.

Today, notice how following Christ is changing you. Thank Him for that work in progress.

What part of your heart is He gently trying to transform? Are you letting Him?

March 6

> *"And he said to them all, If any man will come after me, let him deny himself, and take up his cross daily, and follow me."*
>
> Luke 9:23

Discipleship isn't just about what you give up. It's about what you take on. Christ invites us to carry our crosses daily. That means facing trials with faith, choosing obedience even when it's inconvenient, and trusting Him with burdens we can't fully carry alone.

The cross you carry might be unseen. A private sorrow. A quiet sacrifice. A calling that stretches you. But when carried with Christ, even the heaviest cross can become holy.

One brother shared that for years, his "cross" was loving a family member who had walked away from the gospel. "I couldn't fix it," he said. "But I could love. And I could trust." That daily choice deepened his discipleship more than any calling ever had.

The Savior's path includes weight. But it also includes power.

Today, identify the cross you are carrying. Invite the Savior to help you carry it with grace.

What would it look like to carry your burdens not alone, but alongside Christ?

March 7

> *"Ye shall know them by their fruits ..."*
> Matthew 7:16

Following Christ is more than something we say. It's something we show. Through kindness, integrity, and quiet faith, our lives become testimonies. And often, the most powerful witness we give isn't loud. It's steady.

A disciple's strength lies not in perfection, but in persistence. In living the gospel when it's hard. In forgiving when it hurts. In choosing faith again after a fall. That kind of life points to Christ without needing to announce it.

One sister shared how her grandfather, who rarely spoke in church, bore his testimony by the way he lived. "He was honest, humble, and always helping someone. Everyone felt the gospel was real around him," she said. His quiet consistency made it easy to believe in goodness, and even easier to believe in God.

You may never know who is being strengthened by your example. But Christ does.

Today, let your discipleship speak through your actions. Live so that others feel His love through you.

What part of your life could bear a clearer testimony of Christ, even without words?

March 8

> *"And now behold, I say unto you, that the thing which will be of the most worth unto you will be to declare repentance unto this people, that you may bring souls unto me ..."*
> Doctrine and Covenants 15:6

Discipleship isn't just personal. It's also purposeful. When we follow Christ, we naturally want to bring others with us. We don't have to be perfect to testify. We just need to be willing.

Sharing the gospel doesn't always mean formal lessons or missionary tags. It can be as simple as living with light. Being kind when it's hard. Offering truth when someone is searching. People are drawn to sincerity and peace. Both grow in discipleship.

One young adult said she started praying each day to be placed in someone's path. "It wasn't dramatic," she said. "Sometimes it was just a small conversation or a chance to listen. But I felt like I was walking with Him."

To follow Christ is to be part of His work. And He will magnify even your smallest efforts.

Today, ask for a chance to share His light in a natural, personal way. Be open to the moment.

What quiet opportunities might the Lord be giving you to bring someone closer to Him?

March 9

> *"And Jesus increased in wisdom and stature, and in favour with God and man."*
>
> Luke 2:52

Even the Savior's mortal journey was one of growth. Though He was perfect, He still experienced learning, patience, and progress. That example teaches us something powerful, "Discipleship is a process."

We often want spiritual growth to be quick and obvious. But more often, it's quiet. It happens in small decisions. In moments of prayer when no one else sees. In choosing to stay faithful even when you feel stretched.

One mission leader said he began writing down one way he had seen growth in himself each week. "It helped me stop focusing on what I hadn't done yet," he said, "and start seeing how Christ was already changing me."

Discipleship is a daily becoming. It's less about where you are and more about where you're headed, with Christ at the center.

Today, recognize one area where you're growing. Give yourself grace for the process.

How is Christ helping you increase in wisdom, faith, or spiritual strength right now?

March 10

> *"If ye love me, keep my commandments."*
> John 14:15

Obedience isn't about strict rule-following. It's about love. When our hearts are turned to Christ, keeping His commandments becomes more than a duty. It becomes a desire.

Christ never asked for shallow compliance. He asked for real devotion. He taught that love and obedience are intertwined. When we love Him, we trust Him. And when we trust Him, we follow where He leads. Even when we don't fully understand.

One teenager shared that she once struggled with a particular standard of the gospel. "I didn't get it," she said. "But I kept trying. I prayed and asked Heavenly Father to help me want to obey. And eventually, I did understand. But more than that, I felt closer to Christ."

Obedience draws us to the Savior. It tunes our hearts to His voice and opens our lives to His peace.

Today, choose one commandment to keep more fully out of love for Christ. Let that love guide you.

Where is Christ inviting you to obey more deeply, not out of fear, but out of devotion?

March 11

> *"And we talk of Christ, we rejoice in Christ,
> we preach of Christ, we prophesy of Christ, ..."*
> 2 Nephi 25:26

True discipleship keeps Christ at the center. It's not just about fitting Him into a busy life. It's about building your life around Him. Every part of your day can be a place for Him to dwell.

When we talk of Christ, we invite His Spirit. When we rejoice in Him, we find joy even in trials. And when we preach of Him, whether with words or quiet example, we point others to the source of all peace.

One father said that simply starting family prayer again changed the feeling in their home. "It wasn't perfect," he said. "But it brought Christ back to the center. And we all felt it."

Discipleship isn't about a checklist. It's about a focus. And when Christ is your focus, everything begins to align.

Today, bring Christ into one part of your routine more intentionally: your conversations, your study, your service.

> **How can you more consistently keep Christ at the center of your day-to-day life?**

March 12

> *"... but be thou an example of the believers, in word, in conversation, in charity, in spirit, in faith, in purity."*
>
> 1 Timothy 4:12

Discipleship shows up in the details. It appears in how we speak, how we act, and how we treat others when no one's watching. It's less about grand gestures and more about quiet consistency.

Christlike living isn't meant to impress. It's meant to reflect. When others see your life, they should catch glimpses of Him through your kindness, your patience, and your steady faith. You don't need a spotlight to make a difference. You just need to live with light.

One Relief Society president said she often wondered if her efforts mattered. "But then someone told me, 'Just being around you makes me feel closer to God.' That changed everything. I realized discipleship was working."

When you live your faith sincerely, people notice. And they remember how they felt in your presence.

Today, choose to be an example of the believers. Let your life speak of Christ, even without words.

Which part of your daily example could better reflect your discipleship right now?

March 13

"Take my yoke upon you, and learn of me; for I am meek and lowly in heart: and ye shall find rest unto your souls."

Matthew 11:29

Discipleship isn't just about doing more. It's about walking with Christ. His yoke is not meant to burden, but to balance. When you link your life with His, you don't carry things alone.

Learning of Christ is a gentle process. It's choosing to study His words, to walk in His ways, and to let His Spirit change you. It's asking in prayer, "What can I learn from Thee today?"

One young woman said she pictured her day like a cart full of responsibilities. "When I tried to push it alone, it always felt too heavy," she said. "But when I imagined Christ helping me push and pull, even the hard things became lighter."

To follow Him is to learn from Him. And every lesson learned in His presence leads to more peace.

Today, invite Christ to walk beside you in one task. Learn from His example as you go.

What part of your day could feel lighter if you shared it with the Savior?

March 14

> *"... that by small and simple things are great things brought to pass; ..."*
>
> Alma 37:6

Discipleship is often quiet. It grows in the moments no one else sees. In early morning prayers. In choosing patience when you feel tired. In remembering Christ during your everyday routine.

We sometimes expect spiritual progress to feel dramatic. But the Lord works gently. He builds us through repetition and small acts of faith. He sees the power in the things that feel too ordinary to matter.

One man said he began reading a single verse each morning, just one, because that was all he felt he could manage. Over time, that small habit became a source of daily peace. "It didn't change my schedule," he said, "but it changed my spirit."

Great things begin with small, faithful efforts.

Today, choose one small act that draws you closer to Christ. Let it be simple and sincere.

What is one small spiritual habit you could begin or renew today?

March 15

> *"Let us put our faith in the Lord Jesus Christ into action!"*
>
> President Russell M. Nelson

Discipleship is lived in ordinary hours. It is making dinner with a prayer in your heart. It is answering a call with kindness. It is going about your daily tasks with a quiet desire to do good.

You do not have to be in a holy place to live a holy life. The Lord sanctifies the simple moments when your heart is turned to Him.

One mother said she used to feel like her discipleship was on pause while she raised her children. "But then I realized folding laundry and cleaning up spills were chances to serve like Christ. I stopped waiting for quiet time and started finding Christ in the chaos."

Every day offers a hundred small chances to follow the Savior.

Today, look for one ordinary task where you can invite Christ in. Let it become an act of devotion.

How can you follow Christ more fully in the unnoticed moments of your day?

March 16

> *"Therefore, hold up your light that it may shine unto the world. Behold I am the light which ye shall hold up ..."*
>
> 3 Nephi 18:24

When we follow Christ, we carry His light. It may not always feel bright or bold, but it is real. And the world needs it, especially the quiet kind of light that comes from steady discipleship.

Your light shines when you forgive quickly. When you speak gently. When you respond to stress with faith. You don't need to be the loudest voice to be a powerful influence. You just need to be filled with the, "Light of the World."

One young man said he started praying each morning, "Help me reflect Your light today." That simple prayer changed the way he interacted with friends, teachers, even strangers. "It made me more aware of how I could lift someone," he said.

Light doesn't force itself. It invites. And it grows brighter every time we choose to follow Him.

Today, pray for the courage to reflect Christ's light wherever you are. Look for one way to lift someone.

How can your light become a quiet testimony of the One you follow?

March 17

> *"Behold, the Lord requireth the heart and a willing mind;..."*
> Doctrine and Covenants 64:34

The Savior isn't looking for perfect people. He is looking for willing hearts. He asks us to come as we are and trust that He can shape something beautiful from our offering.

Discipleship begins with a desire to follow. You may not always feel ready. You may not always feel strong. But if you are willing, the Lord will work with you. He honors every honest effort and magnifies even small acts of obedience.

One new convert said she didn't feel like she knew enough to be a good disciple. "But I just kept saying yes," she said. "Yes to reading. Yes to praying. Yes to trying again. And over time, I stopped feeling like a beginner and started feeling like I belonged."

The Lord meets you where you are. What He asks is your heart.

Today, offer Him your willingness. Trust that He can make more of your effort than you can.

Where might the Lord be asking for your heart and a willing mind right now?

March 18

> *"And blessed are they who do hunger and thirst after righteousness: for they shall be filled with the Holy Ghost."*
>
> 3 Nephi 12:6

Discipleship begins with desire. You don't have to know everything or have it all figured out. You just have to want what is good. When you truly hunger for the things of God, He will meet you with abundance.

Hungering after righteousness means craving more than just knowledge. It means seeking the Spirit, longing for truth, and desiring to live in a way that draws you closer to Christ. It's a yearning that turns into action.

One missionary shared that she started her days by simply praying, "Help me want what You want." That small shift changed how she studied, how she served, and how she felt. "I stopped chasing approval and started seeking peace," she said.

When you hunger for the things of God, He fills you in ways the world never could.

Today, ask the Lord to help you hunger more for what is right. Let that desire lead your choices.

What are you spiritually hungering for right now, and how is the Lord helping to fill you?

March 19

> *"Yea, and cry unto God for all thy support;..."*
> Alma 37:36

Discipleship is more than tasks. It is connection. One of the most powerful ways to follow Christ is to stay in constant communication with Him through prayer.

Not all prayers need to be long. Sometimes it is just a few honest words in your mind as you go about your day. Sometimes it is a deep sigh heavenward when you don't know what to say. The Lord listens to all of it.

One woman said she started thinking of prayer as a conversation she kept open throughout the day. "I stopped waiting for the perfect moment. I just included Him in the small, everyday moments. It helped me feel closer to heaven in the middle of everything."

When your heart turns to the Lord often, your life begins to turn with it. That is the rhythm of discipleship.

Today, practice drawing your heart out in prayer. Talk to the Lord in quiet moments. Let Him stay close.

What would it look like for you to keep a prayer in your heart throughout the day?

March 20

> *"Wherefore, be faithful; stand in the office which I have appointed unto you; succor the weak, lift up the hands which hang down, and strengthen the feeble knees."*
> Doctrine and Covenants 81:5

Discipleship includes standing faithfully in your place. That might be a calling, a role in your family, or a quiet responsibility no one else sees. Whatever your post, the Lord needs you there and He will strengthen you to fulfill it.

Sometimes we feel too small to make a difference. But the Lord doesn't measure by size. He sees faithfulness. He sees the one who shows up, who lifts others, who stays steady even when it's hard.

One deacon's quorum adviser said he used to wonder if the boys were listening. "But one day, years later, one of them said, 'I always noticed you were there.' That was enough for me."

Being dependable in discipleship blesses more than you know.

Today, stand faithfully in your place. Trust that your steady presence matters.

Where has the Lord appointed you right now, and how can you serve with more purpose?

March 21

> *"... for ye have not come thus far save it were by the word of Christ with unshaken faith in him, ..."*
>
> 2 Nephi 31:19

Discipleship is a journey. And sometimes, the only way to see how far you have come is to look back. You may not feel different from one day to the next, but grace has been at work in you. Faith has been growing, even in the quiet.

Every step you've taken toward Christ matters. Every prayer whispered in doubt. Every scripture read when you were tired. Every act of obedience, even when it felt small. These moments are not forgotten by the Lord.

One sister said she often felt like she wasn't progressing fast enough. But then she started keeping a spiritual journal. "Looking back, I saw patterns. I saw how the Lord had been changing me little by little. That perspective gave me peace."

Discipleship isn't about speed. It's about direction. And if you are still walking with Christ, you are still moving forward.

Today, reflect on your journey. Notice the quiet ways the Lord has helped you grow.

What spiritual progress have you made that you didn't recognize in the moment?

March 22

> *"And he saith unto them, Follow me, and I will make you fishers of men."*
>
> Matthew 4:19

The call to follow Christ is simple, but it changes everything. When the Savior invited the fishermen to follow Him, He wasn't just asking them to leave their boats. He was inviting them into a new identity, a new purpose, and a new way of life.

That same invitation still stands. To follow Christ is to let go of old ways and step into something higher. You may not know exactly where He will lead, but you can trust who is leading you.

One man said he used to fear what discipleship might cost him. "But the more I followed Christ, the more I realized I wasn't losing anything that mattered. I was gaining peace, purpose, and a deeper connection with God."

Discipleship always begins with a choice. And every time you choose Christ, you are becoming more like Him.

Today, choose to follow Him again. Let go of one thing that no longer serves your soul.

What does following Christ look like in your life right now? What might He be asking you to leave behind?

March 23

> *"Learn of me, and listen to my words; walk in the meekness of my Spirit, and you shall have peace in me."*
>
> Doctrine and Covenants 19:23

Discipleship means becoming a student of the Savior. Not just learning about Him, but learning *from* Him. His life is the lesson. His Spirit is the teacher. And peace is the promised result.

The world often teaches that strength is loud, bold, and self-promoting. But Christ teaches something different. He teaches meekness, gentleness, and quiet trust. These are not signs of weakness. They are signs of discipleship.

One young adult said she began studying the Gospels to better understand Christ's personality. "I wanted to see how He treated people, how He responded to pressure. The more I studied, the more I wanted to be like Him, not just believe in Him."

To follow Christ is to pattern your life after His. And in doing so, you'll find a peace that outlasts your circumstances.

Today, study one story or teaching of Jesus. Learn something from Him and about Him.

What aspect of Christ's character do you feel drawn to learn more about right now?

March 24

> *"Draw near unto me and I will draw near unto you; ..."*
>
> Doctrine and Covenants 88:63

Christ doesn't wait for perfect conditions before He draws near. He responds to sincere desire. If you take one step toward Him, He takes many toward you. That's the kind of Savior He is.

Drawing near doesn't always require big changes. Sometimes it starts with a heartfelt prayer, a moment of stillness, or a renewed effort to listen to the Spirit. The Lord honors each attempt.

One woman said she made a goal to spend five minutes a day with her scriptures. "It didn't feel like much at first," she said. "But over time, I felt something shift. My day felt different. My heart felt softer. I knew I was drawing nearer."

Discipleship is not about perfection. It is about proximity. And the closer you get to Christ, the more you feel His peace.

Today, take one step closer to the Savior. Even a small move toward Him will be met with grace.

What is one simple way you can draw nearer to Christ today?

March 25

> *"By this shall all men know that ye are my disciples, if ye have love one to another."*
> John 13:35

The clearest sign of discipleship is love. Not just love in theory, but love in action. Love that shows up in how we speak, how we forgive, how we listen, and how we serve.

To follow Christ is to love like He did. With patience. With compassion. Without keeping score. And even when it is hard.

One sister said she started pausing before she responded to frustrating situations and asking herself, "What would love do right now?" That small shift changed her tone, her choices, and her relationships. "I didn't always get it right," she said, "but I always felt closer to Christ when I tried."

Discipleship isn't proven through perfect behavior. It is shown through Christlike love.

Today, let love be your answer. Let it guide your words and soften your reactions.

Where can you show more of the Savior's love in your daily interactions?

March 26

> "And behold, I am the light and the life of the world; ..."
>
> 3 Nephi 11:11

When you choose to follow Christ, you are choosing light. It may not remove every shadow from your life, but it will show you the way through. His light brings clarity, comfort, and courage.

There will be moments when darkness feels close. These may be moments of confusion, discouragement, or fear. But even then, His light is not far. It reaches gently, steadily, and personally. All He asks is that you turn toward it.

One man said he kept a small picture of Christ near his bedside. "Each morning, it reminded me to begin in the light. Even on hard days, it helped me remember who I was following."

Discipleship doesn't promise an easy road. It promises a lighted one.

Today, seek the light of Christ in one quiet moment. Let it remind you who you are walking with.

How do you notice His light guiding your path, even in small ways

March 27

> *"Then said Jesus unto his disciples, If any man will come after me, let him deny himself, and take up his cross, and follow me."*
>
> Matthew 16:24

Following Christ isn't always convenient. It often asks us to choose faith over comfort, humility over pride, and obedience over ease. But every sacrifice made to follow Him leads to something better.

Taking up your cross can look different each day. Some days, it means forgiving someone who hurt you. Other days, it means choosing prayer over distraction or trusting God's plan when you cannot see the outcome.

One young adult said that as she tried to follow the Savior more fully, she realized it wasn't about one big, dramatic moment. "It was a hundred small choices to be faithful when no one was watching. That's what changed me."

Discipleship is not a one-time decision. It is a daily devotion.

Today, choose to carry your cross with courage. Let each small act of faith draw you closer to the Savior.

What does taking up your cross look like in your life today?

March 28

> *"He that hath my commandments, and keepeth them, he it is that loveth me: and he that loveth me shall be loved of my Father, and I will love him, ..."*
>
> John 14:21

Obedience is one of the purest expressions of love for the Savior. It's not about checking boxes or earning favor. It's about aligning your heart with His will because you trust Him and want to walk in His ways.

Following commandments doesn't always feel grand or spiritual. Sometimes it looks like honesty when it would be easier to lie. It looks like integrity when no one is watching. It looks like choosing the harder right instead of the easier wrong.

One seminary student said he started asking himself, "What would it look like to love Christ in this moment?" That simple question changed how he made decisions. "It stopped being about rules and started being about relationship."

Obedience is love in action. It turns belief into behavior and commitment into covenant living.

Today, show your love for the Savior through one act of quiet obedience. Let it be sincere.

How can obedience become more of a love offering than a checklist in your discipleship?

March 29

> "O then, my beloved brethren, come unto the Lord, the Holy One. Remember that his paths are righteous..."
>
> 2 Nephi 9:41

Sometimes following Christ means stepping into the unknown. You may not see the full path ahead, but you can trust the One who walks it with you. His ways are sure, even when your vision is not.

Faithful discipleship isn't always about having all the answers. It's about having enough trust to take the next step. It's walking forward when it would be easier to stand still.

One man shared how he felt prompted to change careers, even though it was risky. "I didn't have certainty, but I had peace. And that peace was enough to help me move forward with faith."

Christ's path is not always easy, but it is always right. And when you follow Him, you are never alone.

Today, take one step forward in faith. Trust that the Lord will guide you where you need to be.

What is one decision where you can follow the Savior's prompting, even if the outcome isn't clear yet?

March 30

> *"I am the good shepherd: the good shepherd giveth his life for the sheep."*
>
> John 10:11

The Savior does not lead from afar. He walks beside you, knowing your name, your needs, and your heart. As the Good Shepherd, He is deeply personal in His care and constant in His guidance.

Discipleship means learning to trust His voice. It means following where He leads, even when the terrain feels unfamiliar or steep. His path may not always be the one you expected, but it is the one that leads to peace.

One woman said that when she was facing a hard decision, she prayed to hear the Shepherd's voice more clearly. "The answer didn't come all at once," she said. "But I felt gently led, step by step, in the direction of hope."

The Shepherd's voice is never harsh or rushed. It is steady, loving, and always inviting you closer.

Today, listen for His voice. Trust that He knows the way, even if you do not.

What does following the Good Shepherd look like in your life today?

March 31

> "And now, my beloved brethren, I would that ye should come unto Christ, who is the Holy One of Israel, and partake of his salvation, and the power of his redemption ..."
>
> Omni 1:26

The call to follow Christ is also a call to come unto Him, again and again. Not just once in a dramatic moment, but daily, quietly, with a heart that seeks Him.

Discipleship is not about arriving at a finish line. It is about returning to the Savior in each season of life. When you're strong, He walks with you. When you're weak, He carries you. In every case, He invites you closer.

One sister said she used to think she had to prove her worth before coming to Christ. "But then I realized, He's the reason I have worth. I come to Him not because I'm perfect, but because I'm His."

Following Him means choosing Him every day. In the small moments. In the hard choices. In the unseen effort to keep your heart soft and your spirit willing.

Today, come unto Christ again. Let Him remind you that He's never stopped walking with you.

What helps you return to the Savior, not just once, but every day?

April

Remember Jesus Christ with a grateful heart, especially through His Atonement and sacred ordinances.

April 1

> *"... This is my body which is given for you: this do in remembrance of me."*
>
> Luke 22:19

As April begins, hearts and minds turn toward Easter. It's a season of reverence and renewal, a time to reflect deeply on the Savior's sacrifice and love. And it begins with a simple invitation: Remember Him.

Christ's plea at the Last Supper wasn't just about that night. It was about every day that would follow. He knew we would need reminders. He knew that in the busyness of life, we'd sometimes forget who we are and what matters most.

One young woman said she started using the sacrament as a personal reset each week. "I used to just think about my sins," she said. "Now I try to focus on the Savior. I ask myself, *What did He do for me this week? And how can I walk with Him in the week ahead?*" That shift helped her feel more peace, more purpose, and more love.

Remembering Christ isn't passive. It changes how we live.

Today, remember Him not just with your thoughts, but with your actions. Let His sacrifice shape your choices.

What does it mean to you to truly remember Christ in your daily life?

April 2

> *"Yea, and as often as my people repent will I forgive them their trespasses against me."*
> Mosiah 26:30

The miracle of the Atonement is not just that Christ forgives, but that He forgives *often*. His mercy is not measured in limited supply. It is extended every time we return to Him, honestly, humbly, and with a heart willing to change.

Repentance isn't about shame. It's about connection. It's a way of returning to Christ, of realigning your soul with His grace. And it's available as often as you need it.

One young man said he used to dread repentance, imagining it was a sign of failure. "But now I see it as an invitation," he said. "It's how I come back to Christ when I've wandered. And every time I do, I feel more whole."

The Savior didn't suffer once so you could be forgiven once. He suffered so you could be healed *whenever* you turn to Him.

Today, remember that Christ's mercy is real, and it is yours. Repentance is not a detour, it is the path back to Him.

How can remembering the Savior's mercy change the way you approach repentance?

April 3

> "For I, the Lord, will forgive whom I will forgive, but of you it is required to forgive all men."
>
> Doctrine and Covenants 64:10

To remember Christ is to remember how He forgives. Freely. Fully. Without holding on to offenses or keeping score. And as His disciples, we are asked to forgive in the same way.

Forgiveness doesn't always come quickly. Sometimes it is a process that requires time, prayer, and repeated effort. But every step you take toward forgiveness invites healing. Not just for the one you are forgiving, but for you.

One woman said she prayed for years to let go of a hurt that lingered. "I kept waiting to feel ready," she said. "But then I realized, I just needed to begin. As soon as I took that step, I felt the Savior meet me with strength I didn't have on my own."

Forgiveness is not a weakness. It is one of the strongest expressions of Christlike love.

Today, consider who the Lord might be inviting you to forgive. Begin with prayer and let Him help your heart soften.

How can remembering the Savior's forgiveness help you extend that same mercy to others?

April 4

> *"My dear young friends, If the Savior were here right now, what would He say to you? I believe He would start by expressing His deep love for you."*
>
> Elder Dieter F. Uchtdorf

Sometimes the simplest truths are the ones we most need to remember. Jesus Christ loves you. Not for what you've done, or failed to do. Not because you've earned it. But because it is who He is.

His love is not distant or theoretical. It is personal. It reaches into the details of your life and offers peace that cannot be replicated by anything else in the world.

One woman said she began each day by whispering, "Jesus loves me." At first, it felt small. But over time, that phrase shifted her whole day. "I didn't just believe He loved me. I started to live like it was true."

Remembering Christ means remembering His love. And when you let that truth settle into your soul, it changes everything.

Today, pause and receive His love. Let it speak louder than your doubts. Let it become your beginning point.

How would your thoughts, actions, and decisions change if you truly remembered how deeply the Savior loves you?

April 5

> *"And we talk of Christ, we rejoice in Christ, we preach of Christ, we prophesy of Christ. ..."*
> 2 Nephi 25:26

To remember Christ is not only a personal act, it is also a shared one. We speak His name with reverence. We rejoice in His promises. We look for opportunities to bring Him into our conversations and our daily thoughts.

Remembering the Savior isn't limited to Sunday worship or quiet scripture study. It happens when you choose to be kind instead of impatient, when you speak hope instead of criticism, and when you testify quietly through the way you live.

One young man said he started ending his journal entries with a sentence about the Savior. "Sometimes it was a simple thank you. Sometimes it was a reminder of what He helped me through that day. Either way, it kept Him at the center of my story."

Christ should not be just a part of your life. He should be the heart of it.

Today, speak of Christ in some way. Say His name in gratitude, in prayer, or in testimony.

What helps you keep Christ at the center of your life and conversations?

April 6

> *"And now, after the many testimonies which have been given of him, this is the testimony, last of all, which we give of him: That he lives!"*
>
> The Living Christ; The Testimony of the Apostles

April 6 marks a sacred anniversary. According to revelation, it is the date of the Savior's birth and the organization of His restored Church in the latter days. It is a day to remember Him with reverence and rejoicing.

He lives. That truth changes everything. Because He lives, there is hope beyond sorrow, peace in uncertainty, and healing for every wound. His Resurrection was not the end of His ministry. It was the beginning of everything that gives life meaning.

One sister shared that she takes time each year on April 6 to read *The Living Christ*. "It reminds me that He is not just a figure of the past. He is my present and my future," she said.

Today is a day to remember the living Christ. To honor Him by living with faith, gratitude, and love.

Today, read or listen to *The Living Christ*. Let it help you remember that the Savior is not distant. He is near, and He is real.

What does it mean to you that Christ lives, not just in history, but in your life today?

April 7

> *"... That they may always have his Spirit to be with them. Amen."*
> Sacrament Prayer, Doctrine and Covenants
> 20:77

The sacrament is more than a tradition. It is a holy invitation. Each week, you are offered the chance to renew your commitment to Christ and receive His Spirit more fully into your life.

It is easy to let the ordinance become routine. The bread and water are passed, the prayers are spoken, and the minutes move quickly. But when you pause to truly remember the Savior, something changes. His peace enters. His love softens your heart. His strength steadies your soul.

One young adult said she started closing her eyes during the sacrament and imagining Christ beside her. "I pictured Him holding out His hand to me. It made the sacrament feel less like a ritual and more like a relationship."

The promise of always having His Spirit is not small. It is one of the greatest gifts of discipleship.

Today, prepare your heart for the sacrament. Think about how you can come to the table with more reverence and love.

> **What helps you focus more deeply on the Savior during the sacrament and feel closer to Him as you worship?**

April 8

> *"And he shall go forth, suffering pains and afflictions and temptations of every kind. ... he will take upon him the pains and the sicknesses of his people."*
>
> Alma 7:11

The Savior did not just suffer for sin. He suffered for sorrow. For sickness. For loneliness. For every silent struggle you carry.

His Atonement was both infinite and intimate. It reached into every part of mortality so that He could comfort you in yours. When you remember Him, you are not only remembering a Redeemer. You are remembering a Friend who understands your path completely.

One man shared that during a long illness, he felt distanced from everyone around him. "But then I realized Christ had already walked this road. I wasn't alone. I was known."

To remember Christ is to remember that He knows what you are going through and that He is walking it with you.

Today, bring your burdens to the Savior. Trust that He has already felt them and stands ready to help you through.

How does knowing Christ has suffered for your specific pain help you feel closer to Him?

April 9

"Greater love hath no man than this, that a man lay down his life for his friends."
                                    John 15:13

The Atonement of Jesus Christ is the greatest act of love the world has ever known. It was not just an offering of life. It was an offering of heart, will, and divinity, all given for you.

Christ did not suffer and die because He had to. He did it because He loves you. His love is not conditional. It is not earned. It is constant, personal, and eternal.

One woman said that whenever she felt unworthy of love, she would picture Christ on the cross thinking of her by name. "It reminded me that I am not forgotten," she said. "I am loved by the One who gave everything for me."

Remembering the Atonement is not meant to make you feel guilty. It is meant to remind you how deeply you are valued.

Today, thank the Savior for His love. Let it guide your thoughts, your choices, and your sense of worth.

What can you do today to live in a way that honors Christ's sacrifice for you?

April 10

> *"Come unto me, all ye that labour and are heavy laden, and I will give you rest."*
> Matthew 11:28

The Savior's invitation is simple and tender. Come unto Him. Not when you have it all figured out, but now. Not when you are strong, but when you are weary. His rest is not just physical. It is a spiritual peace that calms the soul.

Sometimes remembering Christ means remembering to turn to Him in the moment. In frustration. In exhaustion. In fear. When life feels too heavy, He offers a place to lay your burden.

One sister shared how she started whispering "Come unto Christ," whenever she felt overwhelmed. "It reminded me that I didn't have to carry it all," she said. "He was willing to carry it with me."

The Savior never waits for you to be perfect. He meets you in your need and offers you His strength.

Today, come unto Christ in prayer. Bring Him your heart, your heaviness, and your hopes. Let Him give you rest.

What part of your life most needs the peace that only Christ can give?

April 11

> *"... as ye are desirous to come into the fold of God, and to be called his people, and are willing to bear one another's burdens, that they may be light."*
>
> Mosiah 18:8

To follow Christ is to remember how He bore burdens. Not just through His suffering in Gethsemane, but through His daily ministry. He lifted others through healing, listening, comforting, and walking beside them.

When you bear one another's burdens, you are not just being kind. You are being Christlike. You are helping someone feel remembered, valued, and loved.

One woman said she felt overwhelmed until a friend dropped off a note and a loaf of bread. "It was small," she said. "But it felt like the Savior saw me. That note reminded me I wasn't alone."

The Atonement is personal, but it also calls you to action. Christ invites you to help carry what others cannot hold by themselves.

Today, look for someone who might need help, even if they never ask. Let the Savior guide you to who needs His love through you.

How can you help bear someone's burden and remind them that Christ has not forgotten them?

April 12

> *"Learn of me, and listen to my words; walk in the meekness of my Spirit, and you shall have peace in me."*
>
> Doctrine and Covenants 19:23

Peace does not come from control or certainty. It comes from Christ. When we remember Him, we remember that true peace is not the absence of trials but the presence of the Savior in the midst of them.

He invites us to learn of Him. To sit at His feet, study His life, and walk in His Spirit. Meekness is not weakness. It is a quiet trust in God that grows stronger even when life is difficult.

One man said he kept this verse on his bathroom mirror. "I saw it every morning and every night. It helped me remember that peace is possible, even when my life feels far from peaceful."

The Savior is not a distant figure. He is a living source of calm in chaos, hope in discouragement, and strength in weakness.

Today, take a moment to quietly sit with the Savior's words. Let them bring peace to your heart.

What can you do to walk more fully in the meekness of His Spirit today?

April 13

> *"During the sacrament we can feel forgiven of our sins."*
>
> Elder Don R. Clarke

The sacrament is not just a symbol. It is a sacred exchange. We offer our hearts, and He offers His healing. We bring our desire to change, and He brings His power to transform.

Each week, this simple ordinance becomes a powerful reminder that the Atonement is ongoing. It does not just cover your past. It fuels your future. It invites you to return to Christ again and again with the promise that He will meet you there.

One sister said she began receiving the sacrament tray as if she were receiving the Savior Himself. "It changed everything," she said. "I felt more reverence and more hope. I felt His love, not just His forgiveness."

Remembering Him during the sacrament means letting Him into every part of your life, including the places that still need healing.

Today, prepare your heart for the sacrament with a prayer of gratitude and a willingness to be changed.

What does the sacrament mean to you personally? How can it become more sacred in your weekly worship?

April 14

> *"Wherefore, redemption cometh in and through the Holy Messiah; for he is full of grace and truth."*
>
> 2 Nephi 2:6

Redemption is not something we earn. It is something we receive through Jesus Christ. His grace does not just cover your shortcomings. It lifts you. It gives you strength to begin again, even when you feel you have failed.

Remembering Him means remembering what He has already done for you and what He continues to offer every day. His truth brings clarity. His grace brings hope. Together, they form the path that leads you back to Him.

One young woman shared how she used to fear making mistakes. "But when I started to understand grace, I felt free," she said. "Free to try, to grow, and to know that Christ would be with me in the process."

The Savior does not wait for perfection. He walks with you through your progress.

Today, reflect on how Christ's grace has carried you. Let that gratitude shape your day.

How has the Redeemer helped you become more than you could be on your own?

April 15

"Jesus said unto her, I am the resurrection, and the life: he that believeth in me, though he were dead, yet shall he live:"

John 11:25

This is the promise of Easter. Life does not end in the grave. Because of Jesus Christ, there is always more. More life. More hope. More to look forward to beyond what we now see.

The Resurrection is not just a future event. It is a present power. It means that anything broken can be restored. Anything lost can be found. And anyone hurting can be healed.

One man said he clung to this scripture after losing a loved one. "It reminded me that goodbye is not the end. Christ made it possible for us to see each other again. That hope carried me."

To remember Christ is to remember that death has been conquered. Fear has been defeated. And life, through Him, is eternal.

Today, let the promise of resurrection fill you with peace and purpose. Hold on to the hope that Christ has already won.

How does the truth of the Resurrection shape the way you live and love today?

April 16

> *"And they remembered his words,"*
>
> Luke 24:8

After the Resurrection, the women at the empty tomb were reminded of what the Savior had told them. And when they remembered His words, their fear gave way to faith.

Christ speaks truth that brings peace, even when the future feels uncertain. His promises remain steady. His teachings give light. When you remember what He has said, you remember who He is.

One sister said she keeps a small journal where she writes down scriptures or impressions that stand out to her. "When I feel anxious or overwhelmed, I read them again. It helps me hear His voice and feel more grounded."

The words of Christ do not fade. They stay with you. They guide your decisions and steady your steps.

Today, take time to remember something the Savior has said. Let it calm your heart and strengthen your faith.

What words of Christ have brought you peace? How can you keep them closer to your heart?

April 17

> *"Yea, they did remember how great things the Lord had done for them, ..."*
> Alma 62:50

Gratitude is a form of remembrance. When you look back and recognize how the Lord has helped you, your faith grows stronger. You begin to trust that He will continue to guide you.

Sometimes the greatest evidence of God's love is found in small moments. A peaceful feeling during prayer. Strength to face a hard day. A gentle reminder that you are not alone.

One woman shared that she began ending each day by writing down one way she saw the Lord's hand. "At first it was hard to think of anything. But after a few weeks, I started noticing His help more easily. It was always there. I just needed to look."

Remembering the Lord is more than a mental act. It is a spiritual habit that opens your eyes to His presence in your life.

Today, think of one way the Lord has helped you recently. Offer a prayer of thanks and let it deepen your trust.

How can remembering past blessings help you move forward with more faith?

April 18

> "Behold, I have graven thee upon the palms of my hands;..."
>
> Isaiah 49:16

The Savior's love is not distant. It is deeply personal. When He suffered in Gethsemane and died on the cross, it was not just for humanity in general. It was for you. Your name, your life, your needs were known to Him.

To be graven on His hands is a powerful image. It means you are not forgotten. You are not overlooked. You are remembered in every moment of His ministry and mercy.

One young adult said this verse helped her during a time of loneliness. "It reminded me that even if no one else noticed me, Christ did. I mattered to Him. That truth gave me strength to keep going."

Remembering Him also means remembering how fully He remembers you.

Today, let this verse remind you how much you matter to the Savior. You are not invisible to Him.

What helps you feel remembered by Christ in your daily life?

April 19

> *"And Moses and Aaron said unto all the children of Israel, At even, then ye shall know that the Lord hath brought you out from the land of Egypt:"*
>
> Exodus 16:6

God remembers His people. Always. Even in the wilderness. Even in captivity. Even when they forgot Him, He did not forget them.

That truth still holds today. In your times of wandering, in your moments of doubt, the Lord does not turn away. He remembers His covenants. He remembers your prayers. He remembers you.

One man said that during a season of silence when answers did not come, he held on to one truth. "God knows me. He remembers me. That was enough to help me keep believing."

When you feel forgotten, remember that you are known by the One who never forgets.

Today, remind yourself that God is mindful of you. His silence is never a sign of absence. It is often a moment of preparation.

How does knowing God remembers you help you trust Him more fully?

April 20

> "O remember, remember, my sons, the words which king Benjamin spake unto his people; yea, remember that there is no other way nor means whereby man can be saved, only through the atoning blood of Jesus Christ, ..."
> Helaman 5:9

To remember Christ is to remember His words. His voice calms storms, softens hearts, and brings clarity to confusion. When you keep His teachings close, you walk with more purpose and peace.

Remembering is not passive. It is a daily choice to hold on to truth, to bring it into your thoughts, and to let it shape your actions.

One sister said she started memorizing short phrases from her scripture study. "When I felt anxious or impatient, I would repeat one to myself. It helped me recenter and remember who I wanted to be."

His words are more than lessons. They are lifelines. They can bring you back to Him in the moments you need Him most.

Today, choose one scripture or phrase from Christ and keep it with you. Let it guide your thoughts and choices.

What words of Christ have stayed with you? How have they helped you remember Him?

April 21

> *"And because of the redemption of man, which came by Jesus Christ, they are brought back into the presence of the Lord; ..."*
>
> Mormon 9:33

The Atonement of Jesus Christ is not only about forgiveness. It is about belonging. He does not just cleanse you from sin. He claims you as His.

To be sealed His is to be known, cherished, and prepared for the presence of God. It is a promise that your life is not random. It has a divine direction and an eternal purpose.

One woman shared that during a time of deep spiritual searching, she felt a clear impression during sacrament meeting. "I am His. That was the thought that kept repeating in my mind. It brought more peace than I had felt in a long time."

Remembering Him means remembering who you are to Him. You are not just someone He saved. You are someone He loves completely.

Today, repeat to yourself this simple truth: "I am His." Let that knowledge shape how you pray, how you act, and how you see yourself.

What would change in your day if you truly remembered that you belong to Christ?

April 22

> "... and always remember him, and keep his commandments which he hath given them; that they may always have his Spirit to be with them. Amen."
>
> Sacrament Blessing, Doctrine and Covenants 20:77

The invitation to always remember Christ is more than a Sunday practice. It is a daily devotion. It shows up in the thoughts you hold, the choices you make, and the love you offer.

When you remember Him, you begin to see your life differently. Ordinary tasks become sacred. Small sacrifices become acts of worship. And quiet moments of kindness become echoes of His example.

One brother said he started placing a small picture of Christ on his dashboard. "Every time I drove, I saw His face. It helped me drive with more patience and speak with more compassion. It reminded me who I follow."

Remembering the Savior is not about being perfect. It is about being intentional. It is about turning your heart toward Him throughout your day.

Today, find a simple way to keep Christ in your thoughts. Let that reminder shape how you live.

What helps you remember Christ throughout your ordinary moments?

April 23

> *"When you remember Jesus Christ and earnestly seek and follow Him, He becomes much more than the central character in scripture stories. His divinity and living reality affect your daily decisions, bless you, and* enliven *you to become more like Him. This powerful change begins when you remember Jesus Christ!"*
>
> Elder David A. Bednar

Remembering the Savior is not just about memory. It is about love. When you cherish Christ, His teachings become more than advice. They become your way of life.

To think of Him often is to anchor your heart in heaven while walking through daily life. You might whisper a prayer while doing dishes or pause to notice His blessings in a quiet moment.

One young woman said she made it a goal to ask herself at the end of each day, "Did I remember Him today?" She said that question changed her focus and brought more meaning to her efforts.

To remember Christ is to honor Him with your heart, your habits, and your hope.

Today, pause and consider how you have remembered the Savior this week.

What is one small way you can cherish Christ more deeply today?

April 24

"... this do in remembrance of me."
Luke 22:19

These words, spoken by the Savior at the Last Supper, are simple and sacred. They invite you to remember not only His sacrifice but His presence. His love. His example.

The sacrament is not just a routine. It is a renewal. A moment where heaven meets earth and your heart has a chance to return to Him again. As you partake of the bread and water, you are not just recalling a historical event. You are reconnecting with the living Christ.

One young man said he began to view sacrament meeting as a weekly covenant conversation. "It was no longer just a meeting. It was a moment with the Savior. That shift helped me come with more purpose and leave with more peace."

When you remember Christ, you are reminded that you are never alone. His grace reaches you every time you turn toward Him.

Today, prepare for your next sacrament experience with a heart ready to remember. Let that moment become more sacred.

What can you do this week to make the sacrament more meaningful and personal?

April 25

> *"... that ye do always remember me. And if ye do always remember me ye shall have my Spirit to be with you."*
>
> 3 Nephi 18:7

This promise from the Savior is both simple and profound. If you remember Him, His Spirit will be with you. That companionship brings clarity, comfort, and quiet strength for whatever lies ahead.

Remembering Christ is not just about recalling His life. It is about letting His life influence yours. His mercy can shape your choices. His love can soften your responses. His presence can calm your fears.

One young adult said she began treating her sacrament prayers like personal covenants. "When I said I would always remember Him, I pictured what that could actually look like in my week. It made the promise feel real."

The Spirit comes not through perfection, but through remembrance. When your heart returns to Christ, He always returns to you.

Today, reflect on the promise of having His Spirit with you. Invite that gift into your thoughts and your choices.

What helps you keep the Savior in your heart beyond the sacrament meeting?

April 26

> *"If we have faith in Jesus Christ, the hardest as well as the easiest times in life can be a blessing."*
>
> Elder Henry B. Eyring

Remembering Christ during trials does not always remove the challenge, but it can change the climb. He walks with you. He strengthens your steps. He helps you see beyond what is hard right now.

When life feels heavy, remembering the Savior means remembering His strength. He did not shrink from suffering, and He does not step away from yours. His Atonement was not just for the moments you fall short. It was also for the days you feel worn thin.

One sister said she kept a small picture of Christ taped inside her journal. "Every time I wrote about something hard, I looked at His face and remembered that I was not alone."

He is the One who understands. The One who lifts. And the One who stays.

Today, invite the Savior into your struggles. Let His presence be your strength.

How has remembering Christ helped you endure something difficult with more faith?

April 27

> "... for the right way is to believe in Christ and deny him not; ..."
>
> 2 Nephi 25:28

To believe in Christ is to remember Him. It is to believe that His promises are sure, His mercy is real, and His love is constant. That belief shapes your direction, your priorities, and your hope.

The world offers many voices, but remembering the Savior helps you recognize the voice that truly matters. His words bring life. His path brings peace. His example brings clarity.

One brother said that when he began studying the Savior's life with more focus, his daily choices shifted. "I started asking, 'What would He do in this situation?' It changed how I worked, how I spoke, and how I treated others."

Belief in Christ is not just a feeling. It is a choice to walk with Him, trust Him, and remember Him, especially when life gets complicated.

Today, renew your belief in Christ by acting on something He taught. Let your faith show up in what you do.

What helps you believe in Christ more deeply when your faith is tested?

April 28

> *"Because of the Savior's Atonement, mercy can prevail for those who have repented, and it can allow them to return to the presence of God."*
>
> Elder Quentin L. Cook

The power of the Atonement stretches beyond forgiveness. It brings healing and the promise of reconciliation with God. Mercy is not a one-time gift. It is powerful enough to restore eternity.

Remembering Christ means recognizing that He has opened the way for you to come home. No matter how far you've strayed. His grace heals wounds. His power breaks through guilt. His mercy lifts you into the presence of God.

One sister shared that after years of feeling spiritually distant, she finally accepted forgiveness through the Atonement. "It felt like I had been carried across a river," she said. "I was exhausted, but His grace took me the rest of the way."

To remember Him is to remember how much He wants you with Him and that He has already made the way possible.

Today, reflect on how the Atonement has brought mercy into your life. Let that knowledge encourage you to move forward in faith.

How does knowing mercy is always available help you come closer to Christ today?

April 29

> *"For the Lord taketh pleasure in his people: he will beautify the meek with salvation."*
> Psalm 149:4

These words remind us that Christ rejoices in you. You are not just a follower, you are beloved. His delight is not for perfection. It is for the person He has created and continues to refine.

To remember Him is to know you are cherished, even in your imperfections. His love is not distant, it is personal and joyous. He sees your efforts, your faith, your hope, and He takes pleasure in every step you take toward Him.

One sister shared that on difficult days she would whisper, "He delights in me." It brought a shift. Instead of self-doubt, she felt reassurance. Instead of discouragement, she felt belonging.

Remembering Christ means remembering you are His beloved.

Today, hold onto the truth that the Lord takes pleasure in you. Let that reality shape your worth and your walk.

How would remembering His delight in you change the way you see yourself and your day?

April 30

> "For I have received of the Lord that which also I delivered unto you, That the Lord Jesus the same night in which he was betrayed took bread:"
>
> 1 Corinthians 11:23

This scripture marks the beginning of Paul's reminder to the early Saints of the sacred covenant we renew each week. It reminds us that the Savior instituted the sacrament to ensure we never forget His great sacrifice and love.

The ordinance is meant to link the past with the present. We remember His suffering. We remember His freedom from death. And we remember His promise to be with us always.

One young mother shared that teaching her children the meaning of the sacrament brought new understanding into her own heart. She said, "As I explained why Christ gave His body, I felt gratitude fill every part of me."

Remembering the Savior through the sacrament is a sacred promise to hold Him in your heart and walk with Him throughout your life.

Today, partake of the sacrament with intention. Let the remembrance anchor you in His love.

How can you make the sacrament in the week ahead an ongoing reflection of Christ's Atonement rather than a single moment?

May

Hear the voice of the Lord through stillness, revelation, and the whisperings of the Holy Ghost.

May 1

> *"Our Father knows that when we are surrounded by uncertainty and fear, what will help us the very most is to hear His Son."*
> President Russell M. Nelson

IN TIMES OF CHAOS or confusion, the voice of the Savior is the true compass. Heavenly Father knows our moments of doubt and distress, and He invites us to find clarity by listening to Jesus Christ.

The Holy Ghost is how we hear Him. Not always through dramatic impressions, but often through calm impressions; subtle thoughts, a feeling of peace, a gentle whisper that guides our steps.

One sister said she began asking quietly each morning, "What would You have me hear today?" As she practiced that in prayer, she started noticing more promptings in scripture, more comfort during trials, and more confidence in her quiet decisions.

To hear Him is to let Him speak into your life. It requires stillness, sincerity, and a heart ready to respond.

Today, invite the Spirit to help you hear the voice of Christ. Then obey the very first prompting you recognize.

What is a small way you can practice listening to the Savior today?

May 2

> *"... and after the fire a still small voice."*
> 1 Kings 19:12

God often speaks in quiet ways. After the wind, the earthquake, and the fire, especially after the dramatic moments, His whisper is what reaches the heart. It is the still small voice that Elijah heard in his moment of fear and exhaustion.

Learning to pause and listen is essential for spiritual guidance. The Holy Ghost speaks gently into our souls, offering guidance, peace, and comfort when we let ourselves be still enough to hear Him.

One sister said she began her mornings with five minutes of silence and a simple question: "What do You want me to know today?" In time, she began noticing subtle promptings, gentle nudges, even ideas that brought clarity to her daily decisions.

Hearing the Spirit does not require noise, crowds, or long answers. It requires openness, stillness, and willingness.

Today, spend a few moments in silence. Ask a simple question and then listen. Allow the Spirit to speak.

What might God's gentle whisper be saying to your heart today?

May 3

> *"Howbeit when he, the Spirit of truth, is come, he will guide you into all truth: for he shall not speak of himself; but whatsoever he shall hear, that shall he speak: and he will shew you things to come."*
>
> John 16:13

The Holy Ghost is our divine Teacher and Guide. As disciples of Christ, we are invited not only to listen, but also to follow the Spirit's promptings. He offers insight, peace, and the hope we need in everyday life.

Revelation is not reserved for prophets alone. It comes in personal nudges, still impressions, and moments of spiritual clarity. When you remember to invite the Spirit, He will help you recognize truth and choose wisely.

One sister shared that when she began ending each day by quietly asking, "What would You have me learn tonight?" she began noticing unexpected answers through scripture, prayer, and even a peaceful thought.

Learning to hear the Spirit is an invitation to deeper discipleship. His voice is living. His guidance is personal. And He is always willing to speak to you.

Today, pause for a moment of stillness. Invite the Holy Ghost to guide one decision or thought. Then listen.

What gentle prompting, reassurance, or truth might the Spirit be offering you today?

May 4

"... This is My Beloved Son. Hear him!"
Joseph Smith—History 1:17

These seven words, spoken by God the Father to a 14-year-old boy in a grove of trees, changed the course of history. They are also a personal invitation to you. *Hear Him.* Not just once, but every day. Not just in moments of crisis, but in every part of your life.

To hear the Savior is to recognize His voice among many. It means making space for stillness, turning down the world's volume, and believing that He speaks to individuals just as He did to prophets.

Joseph Smith went into the grove with a question and a heart full of faith. The answer he received not only restored the Church but restored the truth that God still speaks.

One man said, "I used to think revelation was rare. But now I see it is regular if I am listening."

The invitation is the same. The power is real. You can hear Him.

Today, take a moment to pray with a specific question. Ask in faith. Then listen with confidence that He will answer.

What might the Lord be waiting to tell you, if you paused to truly hear Him?

May 5

> *"He that hath ears to hear, let him hear."*
> Matthew 11:15

This scripture is both simple and profound. It is a call to attention. A reminder that hearing the Savior is not just about sound, but about spiritual readiness.

To hear Him, we must tune our hearts to His voice. That often means slowing down, removing distractions, and listening not just with our minds but with our spirits. His voice invites us to peace, to truth, and to change.

One young man said that when he started turning off the noise during his commute—no music, no podcasts—he began to feel more spiritual impressions. "It was like the Lord had been trying to speak," he said, "but I had not been quiet enough to hear Him."

Spiritual hearing takes effort. It is an active choice to make time, ask sincerely, and be ready for answers.

Today, create a quiet moment for the Lord. Turn something off and turn your heart toward Him.

What distractions might you remove this week to better hear the Savior's voice?

May 6

> *"But the Comforter, which is the Holy Ghost, whom the Father will send in my name, he shall teach you all things, and bring all things to your remembrance, whatsoever I have said unto you."*
>
> John 14:26

The Spirit teaches by bringing things to our remembrance. Often, that means truth we already know but have forgotten in the rush of life. He reminds us of Christ's love, of our worth, of the path we are trying to follow.

When you feel a quiet reassurance, a sudden insight, or even a nudge to choose better, that is the Spirit doing His work. His voice is not loud, but it is powerful. It lifts, guides, and corrects with perfect love.

One woman said she kept a journal of spiritual impressions. "Sometimes it was just one sentence," she said, "but over time, I saw patterns. I realized how often the Spirit really was speaking."

You do not need to be perfect to feel the Holy Ghost. You just need to be open, willing, and ready to act.

Today, pay attention to what the Spirit brings to your mind.

How can you make space in your day to better recognize what the Holy Ghost is teaching you?

May 7

"Hearken, O ye people of my church, saith the voice of him who dwells on high, and whose eyes are upon all men; ..."
Doctrine and Covenants 1:1

The very first word in the Doctrine and Covenants is hearken. It is more than just hearing. It means to listen with the intent to obey. To hearken is to receive the word of the Lord and act on it.

In the simple command to "hear Him," God teaches us how to live with clarity and purpose. The Savior speaks to lead us. The Holy Ghost confirms His truth. Our part is to listen and then follow.

One sister missionary said she began asking in prayer, "What is one thing You would have me do today?" As she acted on those impressions, she felt a deeper connection with heaven and more peace in her decisions.

Hearing Him brings light. But hearkening—choosing to obey—brings transformation.

Today, ask in prayer what the Lord would have you do. Then do it. Listen with faith and act with courage.

What does it mean to you to not only hear but also to hearken to the voice of the Lord?

May 8

> *"Yea, behold, I will tell you in your mind and in your heart, by the Holy Ghost, which shall come upon you and which shall dwell in your heart."*
>
> Doctrine and Covenants 8:2

Revelation does not come in only one way. The Lord promises to speak to both mind and heart. That means you may feel truth settle in gently. Or you may understand clearly and suddenly. Both are revelation. Both are real.

Sometimes the Spirit brings peace. Other times it brings urgency or clarity. Each time, it is a message just for you. God speaks in the way you are most likely to hear.

One returned missionary said she always expected to feel something dramatic when praying for answers. But over time she learned that peace, confidence, and recurring thoughts were just as powerful.

When you are in tune with the Spirit, revelation becomes a part of everyday life. It is personal. It is constant. And it is a gift.

Today, ask the Lord to speak to both your heart and your mind. Be open to the quiet ways He may answer.

How has the Holy Ghost spoken to you in the past? How can you recognize His voice again today?

May 9

> *"As we seek to be disciples of Jesus Christ, our efforts to hear Him need to be ever more intentional. It takes conscious and consistent effort to fill our daily lives with His words, His teachings, His truths."*
> President Russell M. Nelson

Hearing the Savior does not happen by accident. It requires intention. It means choosing to make time for His words and teachings each day, even when life feels busy or overwhelming.

To hear Him more clearly, we must create space for stillness. That might mean reading the scriptures with focus. It might mean listening to a conference talk while doing chores. It could be a quiet moment of reflection at the end of the day.

One brother said that when he began setting a five-minute timer for spiritual focus each morning, his mind began to shift. "I used to just start my day in a rush," he said. "Now I start it with purpose."

Intentional discipleship is steady. It is built one choice at a time. And it opens the way to hear Him more often and more clearly.

Today, make one small but deliberate choice to hear the Savior. Let it be a beginning.

What is one way you can intentionally invite the voice of the Lord into your daily routine?

May 10

> *"If thou shalt ask, thou shalt receive revelation upon revelation, knowledge upon knowledge, that thou mayest know the mysteries and peaceable things—that which bringeth joy, that which bringeth life eternal."*
>
> Doctrine and Covenants 42:61

God is not distant. He is a Father who answers. Revelation is available to every seeking soul who turns to Him in faith.

Asking in prayer is the first step. But receiving often comes in quiet moments afterward. Through thoughts, feelings, scriptures, and impressions, the Lord teaches us line upon line. He does not just give us answers. He helps us grow into them.

One returned missionary shared that he used to pray and then rush on with his day. But he learned on his mission that he should pause after his prayers, even for just a minute or two, and he began to sense the Spirit more often. "It was not always dramatic," he said. "But I could feel Him answering."

If you are willing to ask, the Lord is willing to answer.

Today, ask a question in your prayers and then make time to listen. Trust that revelation will come in the way that is right for you.

What question is on your heart today? How can you invite the Lord to teach you line upon line?

May 11

> *"Be still, and know that I am God:..."*
> Psalm 46:10

Stillness is not just the absence of noise. It is a spiritual quieting that allows space for the Lord's voice to be heard. In a world that values constant motion and volume, stillness becomes a sacred act of trust.

To be still is to set aside the distractions. It is to pause, breathe, and remember that God is present. It is choosing calm over chaos and connection over consumption.

One sister said she began setting a timer for two minutes of silence after her scripture study. "At first it felt awkward," she said. "But soon those minutes became the most peaceful part of my day. I started hearing the Spirit more clearly."

Stillness invites clarity. It invites comfort. And it invites revelation.

Today, practice spiritual stillness. Turn off the noise for a few moments and sit with the Lord. Let your heart be quiet enough to hear Him.

What part of your day could be offered as a moment of stillness before the Lord?

May 12

> *"For verily, verily I say unto you, he that hath the spirit of contention is not of me, but is of the devil, who is the father of contention, and he stirreth up the hearts of men to contend with anger, one with another."*
>
> 3 Nephi 11:29

Contention clouds spiritual hearing. When our hearts are stirred by anger, pride, or defensiveness, it becomes harder to feel the gentle promptings of the Holy Ghost. The Spirit dwells in peace, not in conflict.

Christ teaches that His followers are peacemakers. That does not mean avoiding hard things. It means approaching them with a soft heart, a clear mind, and a desire to understand. When we choose peace, we are better able to hear Him.

One sister shared that after a heated argument, she went on a walk to cool down. As she prayed for calm, the Spirit quietly impressed on her heart what she needed to say to reconcile. "I would have missed it if I had stayed angry," she said. "Peace made room for the Spirit."

Hearing Him often begins with choosing peace.

Today, notice how your emotions affect your ability to hear the Spirit. If needed, pray for the peace that invites His voice.

What helps you quiet contention and invite the Spirit into your heart and relationships?

May 13

> "And by the power of the Holy Ghost ye may know the truth of all things."
>
> Moroni 10:5

Truth is not something we discover on our own. It is something revealed to us through the Spirit. The Holy Ghost is not just a comforter. He is a teacher and a testifier. He confirms what is real and right with a feeling deeper than intellect alone.

When the Spirit speaks, it brings light. That light may come as warmth in your heart, clarity in your thoughts, or a peaceful assurance that settles quietly within. However it comes, it is always consistent with truth and always centered in Christ.

One seminary student said she often doubted if she was feeling the Spirit. But when she started writing down the moments when she felt peace, strength, or joy while learning gospel truths, she began to see a pattern. "That was the Spirit," she realized. "He had been there all along."

The Holy Ghost is not silent. He is steady. He teaches truth to those who are ready to receive it.

Today, ask the Lord to help you recognize truth through the Spirit. Be open to how that truth may come.

How have you come to know spiritual truths through the power of the Holy Ghost?

May 14

> *"For my soul delighteth in the song of the heart; yea, the song of the righteous is a prayer unto me, ..."*
>
> Doctrine and Covenants 25:12

Music can be a sacred channel for revelation. It reaches the heart when words fall short. Hymns and spiritual songs often carry the Spirit with power that lifts, softens, and teaches.

When we sing or listen with faith, we open ourselves to the influence of the Holy Ghost. The message of a song can confirm a testimony, bring comfort, or offer an answer we have been seeking. Sometimes, a familiar line will echo in our mind long after the music ends.

One man shared that during a difficult time, he would quietly hum *I Need Thee Every Hour* each morning. "It helped me feel the Lord was near," he said. "That simple song became my daily prayer."

The Lord delights in the songs that rise from a sincere heart. Through them, we often hear Him more clearly.

Today, listen to or sing a hymn that draws you closer to Christ. Pay attention to what the Spirit teaches through it.

What hymn or sacred music helps you feel the presence and voice of the Lord?

May 15

> *"Did I not speak peace to your mind concerning the matter? What greater witness can you have than from God?"*
> Doctrine and Covenants 6:23

Revelation is not always a dramatic moment. Often, it is a quiet reassurance. The Lord's voice brings peace to the mind and clarity to the heart. That peace is personal, powerful, and unmistakable once we learn to recognize it.

We sometimes expect big answers when God is offering simple confirmation. A calm feeling when you pray. A sense of rightness as you move forward. A gentle quiet that replaces confusion. These are all ways He speaks peace.

One college student said she was deciding between two good options and felt unsure. After praying, she still felt no strong impression. But when she moved forward with one of the choices, she felt peace. "That peace was my answer," she said. "It didn't shout. It settled."

When God speaks peace, it is a witness that you are on the right path.

Today, look back on a moment when the Lord spoke peace to your mind. Let that memory strengthen your trust in His voice.

When have you felt the Lord's peace confirming a choice, decision, or direction?

May 16

> *"For God is not the author of confusion, but of peace, ..."*
>
> 1 Corinthians 14:33

When we are overwhelmed, it is easy to mistake anxiety for inspiration. But the Spirit brings clarity, not chaos. God does not speak in a way that leaves us tangled in fear or spinning in indecision. His voice calms, confirms, and directs.

Recognizing the Spirit requires us to slow down and make space for peace. It means learning the difference between urgent noise and quiet truth. That may take time and practice, but the Lord is patient with our learning.

One woman shared that she used to second-guess every impression, unsure if it was from God or just her own thoughts. But as she studied the scriptures and wrote down her impressions, she began to notice a pattern. "The Spirit's voice always brought peace and purpose," she said. "It didn't confuse me. It calmed me."

When you are unsure, seek the voice that brings peace. That is where you will find Him.

Today, if a decision feels confusing or rushed, step back and invite peace. Let that peace help you discern the Lord's voice.

How do you distinguish between the noise of the world and the peace of the Spirit?

May 17

> *"Ask, and it shall be given you; seek, and ye shall find; knock, and it shall be opened unto you:"*
>
> Matthew 7:7

The Lord invites us to be active in our pursuit of revelation. He wants us to ask, to seek, and to knock. That kind of effort shows desire, faith, and trust in His timing. Revelation is not passive. It is a partnership between divine guidance and our willingness to receive.

Sometimes answers come right away. Other times, they unfold slowly. But every sincere prayer opens the door to heaven. Every honest question invites the Lord's help.

One young man said he was struggling with a major decision and felt stuck. After praying, he decided to write down his question and bring it with him to the temple. During his time there, a clear impression came. "It was not just an answer," he said. "It was a reminder that God really is listening."

When you ask in faith, God responds in love.

Today, bring a specific question to the Lord in prayer. Trust that your seeking is sacred and that answers will come.

What do you need to ask, seek, or knock for today? How can you prepare to receive?

May 18

"We simply cannot rely upon information we bump into on social media. With billions of words online and in a marketing-saturated world constantly infiltrated by noisy, nefarious efforts of the adversary, where can we go to hear Him?"
President Russell M. Nelson

There is a difference between being informed and being spiritually grounded. In a world where voices shout from every direction, the voice that matters most can be the hardest to hear. That is why the Lord invites us to seek Him with intention.

To hear Christ, we must make space for Him. That may be by turning off media, choosing to sit with the scriptures, or praying without rushing. The adversary uses noise to confuse. Christ uses stillness to comfort.

One young woman said she started a habit of walking outside each evening without her phone. "That was the first time I realized how much I had been listening to everything else," she said. "Now I use that time to listen for Him."

God still speaks. The question is not whether He is speaking. It is whether we are quiet enough to hear.

Today, turn down the world's volume for a few minutes. Open your heart and ask to hear Him.

What can you remove or adjust in your daily routine to better hear the voice of the Lord?

May 19

> *"But the Comforter, which is the Holy Ghost, whom the Father will send in my name, he shall teach you all things, and bring all things to your remembrance, whatsoever I have said unto you."*
>
> John 14:26

The Holy Ghost is both a teacher and a reminder. He helps us learn truth and remember it when we need it most. He brings back scriptures we studied, lessons we heard, and feelings we felt. That remembrance is often the revelation we need in the moment.

God does not expect us to carry everything perfectly in our minds. He has given us the Spirit to recall, reinforce, and reassure.

One sister shared how a verse from the Book of Mormon came to her mind during a hard day. She had not studied it recently, but it came clearly and brought comfort. "That verse was exactly what I needed," she said. "It reminded me that God is aware of me."

The Spirit often speaks by reminding us what we already know.

Today, ask the Holy Ghost to bring to your remembrance something the Lord has already taught you. Be open to what comes.

When has the Spirit reminded you of something you needed at just the right time?

May 20

> *"The Spirit itself beareth witness with our spirit, that we are the children of God;"*
> Romans 8:16

Personal revelation often begins with personal identity. The Holy Ghost testifies of truth, and one of the first truths He confirms is who you really are. You are a child of God. That knowledge anchors everything else you will ever learn through the Spirit.

When life feels uncertain or your sense of worth is shaken, the Spirit can reaffirm your divine origin and eternal value. That witness can be quiet, but it is powerful.

One youth shared how he had struggled to feel like he belonged at church. During a quiet moment at a youth devotional, the Spirit whispered to his heart, "You are mine." He said, "I did not hear words out loud, but I felt them. And I believed them."

When you know who you are to God, you begin to hear His voice more clearly.

Today, ask the Lord to remind you of your divine identity. Let the Spirit witness again that you are His.

How has the Spirit helped you understand your worth as a child of God?

May 21

> *"Counsel with the Lord in all thy doings, and he will direct thee for good; ..."*
>
> Alma 37:37

Revelation is not reserved for the big moments. It is meant for the daily ones. The Lord invites us to counsel with Him in all things. Not just the spiritual, but the practical, the ordinary, and the personal. He cares about our relationships, responsibilities, and routines.

When you involve the Lord in your everyday life, you begin to see His hand in unexpected places. Guidance does not always come as a clear answer. Sometimes it comes as a quiet nudge or a gentle increase in confidence to move forward.

One woman said she started beginning each day with a simple question in prayer: "What would Thou have me do today?" She said, "It helped me pay attention. I felt more guided and more grateful."

The Lord will direct your steps as you invite Him into the details.

Today, counsel with the Lord about something small. Trust that He is just as present in the ordinary as in the sacred.

What simple part of your life can you invite the Lord to guide today?

May 22

> *"If thou shalt ask, thou shalt receive revelation upon revelation, knowledge upon knowledge, that thou mayest know the mysteries and peaceable things—that which bringeth joy, that which bringeth life eternal."*
> Doctrine and Covenants 42:61

Revelation is not a one-time gift. It is a continuing flow. The more we ask, the more we receive. The more we listen, the more we learn. God is a God of abundance, and He delights in teaching His children.

Sometimes we feel hesitant to ask for more. We worry we are bothering God or that our questions are too small. But the Lord invites us to ask freely and often. Revelation grows with our faith and willingness to seek it.

One brother shared that he once prayed only when things were serious. But as he began to include God in his daily thoughts, impressions started coming more often. "It was like a conversation began," he said. "And I realized He had been waiting to speak all along."

The Lord is generous with revelation when we are ready to receive it.

Today, ask in faith and expect to receive. Let your prayers reflect the trust that God wants to speak to you.

What more could you learn if you trusted that revelation comes one answer at a time?

May 23

"I promise that as you increase your time in temple and family history work, you will increase and improve your ability to hear Him."

President Russell M. Nelson

Sometimes we overlook the connection between sacred service and personal revelation. President Nelson reminds us that the temple is not just a place of worship. It is a place of instruction. As we engage in temple and family history work, the Spirit can speak more clearly to our hearts.

Hearing Him is not always about changing your environment. Often, it is about elevating it. The temple does that. So does searching for ancestors, preparing names, and learning about your family story.

One brother said that while doing family history work, he suddenly felt a distinct impression about a personal decision he had been struggling with. "It had nothing to do with what I was researching," he said, "but I knew the Spirit was speaking to me because I had made space for it."

When you enter the Lord's house or engage in His holy work, you make yourself more available to His voice.

Today, consider doing something that connects you to the temple. It may be as simple as looking up an ancestor or reviewing a recent ordinance.

What spiritual guidance has come to you through temple or family history work?

May 24

> *"But let him ask in faith, nothing wavering. For he that wavereth is like a wave of the sea driven with the wind and tossed."*
>
> James 1:6

Faith is the foundation of revelation. It is not just hoping God will answer. It is believing He will and trusting that He knows how and when to respond. Revelation is often less about receiving a message and more about being ready for it.

When we doubt, we close off possibilities. But when we ask in faith, we open the door to divine instruction. That faith does not have to be perfect. It just needs to be sincere.

A young woman shared how she struggled to feel answers to prayer. But she decided to believe anyway and kept praying each night. One evening, a scripture came clearly to her mind, bringing the peace she had been hoping for. "It came because I chose to believe it could," she said.

Faith is the signal heaven responds to.

Today, pray with the belief that God hears you. Let your faith be the space where revelation begins.

What does it mean to you to ask in faith? How can you show that faith today?

May 25

> *"And by the power of the Holy Ghost ye may know the truth of all things."*
>
> Moroni 10:5

Truth is not discovered by logic alone. It is confirmed by the Spirit. The Holy Ghost teaches truth in a way that goes deeper than explanation. He helps us feel the rightness of a principle, the divinity of a message, and the reality of God's love.

Sometimes the Spirit confirms truth in a moment of study. Other times, it comes in a feeling that stays long after an experience. Either way, that quiet witness is how we come to know.

One man shared how he struggled with a gospel principle for years. But during a quiet prayer, he felt a warmth and clarity he could not explain. "I didn't get all the answers," he said, "but I knew it was true. And that was enough."

Truth recognized by the Spirit becomes truth anchored in the soul.

Today, ask the Holy Ghost to confirm something you are learning or wondering about. Trust the quiet witness He gives.

When has the Holy Ghost helped you know that something was true?

May 26

> *"Be still, and know that I am God: I will be exalted among the heathen, I will be exalted in the earth."*
>
> Psalm 46:10

Stillness is not just the absence of noise. It is the presence of peace. It is a chosen quiet where the Spirit can speak and the soul can listen. In a world that rushes and distracts, stillness becomes sacred space.

Sometimes we expect revelation to break through the chaos. But more often, it comes when we choose to step away from it. The Lord often speaks when we are still enough to hear.

One young man said he started setting aside five minutes a day with no music, no phone, and no noise. "It felt strange at first," he said. "But then I began to feel something. Clarity. Calm. I realized the Spirit had been waiting for me."

Stillness invites revelation in ways that busyness cannot.

Today, make room for stillness. Let the quiet become a place where you hear Him more clearly.

What could you remove or pause today to create a moment of stillness with the Lord?

May 27

> *"We also hear Him more clearly as we refine our ability to recognize the whisperings of the Holy Ghost. It has never been more imperative to know how the Spirit speaks to you than right now."*
>
> President Russell M. Nelson

Learning to hear the Holy Ghost is not a one-time event. It is a lifelong process of spiritual refinement. It means paying attention to how He speaks to you. It means noticing patterns, recording impressions, and acting on even the smallest whisperings.

The world grows louder every day. That makes the whisper of the Spirit more precious than ever before. Knowing how He speaks to you gives you spiritual confidence no matter what is happening around you.

One sister said she keeps a notebook titled "Things the Spirit Taught Me." Each entry is brief, but over time it has become a powerful reminder that God is constantly communicating with her.

The more you listen, the more you recognize. And the more you recognize, the more you trust that you truly can hear Him.

Today, reflect on how the Spirit has spoken to you before. Pray to refine your ability to hear Him.

How does the Holy Ghost speak to you? How can you become more familiar with His voice?

May 28

> *"But the fruit of the Spirit is love, joy, peace, longsuffering, gentleness, goodness, faith,"*
> Galatians 5:22

One of the most consistent ways to recognize the Spirit is by the feelings it brings. Love. Joy. Peace. These are not just emotions. They are evidence that the Spirit is near. The fruits of the Spirit are often the very answers we are seeking.

When we feel uplifted, calm, or more patient, we can trust that the Spirit is working within us. Revelation is not always dramatic. Sometimes it is as simple as a peaceful confirmation to keep going.

One woman said she was struggling to know if she was on the right path. After praying, she felt no voice or vision, but an increase of calm throughout the day. "I did not get a message," she said. "I got peace. And that told me everything I needed to know."

The presence of peace is often the confirmation of truth.

Today, pay attention to the fruits of the Spirit in your life. They may be the Lord's way of answering your prayers.

What fruit of the Spirit do you need most right now? How can you invite it in?

May 29

> *"Did I not speak peace to your mind concerning the matter? What greater witness can you have than from God?"*
>
> Doctrine and Covenants 6:23

Sometimes we ask for more when God has already spoken. We hope for another sign, a louder answer, or clearer direction. But peace is often the confirmation. When the Spirit quiets the fear or lifts the burden, that is revelation.

The peace of God is not always dramatic. It is steady. It reassures without explaining everything. It confirms without revealing the entire path. That kind of peace is a gift and a witness that He is near.

One man said he kept second-guessing a decision, even after feeling peace in prayer. "I kept asking again," he said, "until I realized the peace I had felt was the answer. God had already spoken."

God's peace is not silence. It is a voice of its own.

Today, look back on a moment when peace was your answer. Let that memory remind you of how God speaks.

Is there something in your life where peace has already come, but you have not trusted it yet?

May 30

"... we hear Him as we heed the words of prophets, seers, and revelators."
President Russell M. Nelson

Prophets speak the words of Christ. When we listen to their counsel with faith and a desire to act, we are not just hearing men. We are hearing Him.

Throughout scripture and in our day, the Lord has chosen prophets to guide His people. Their messages are not always dramatic or new. Sometimes they are quiet reminders to stay the course. But when we treat their words as revelation and not suggestion, we will find our lives anchored in truth.

One young woman said she started reading General Conference talks during her scripture study. "At first I did it as a checklist," she said. "But then I started to feel like the Lord was speaking directly to me through their words."

The voice of the Lord often comes through those He has called. As we give heed, our ability to recognize His voice in all its forms increases.

Today, take time to study a recent message from a prophet or apostle. Ask the Lord what He wants you to learn from it.

When have the words of a living prophet helped you hear the voice of the Savior more clearly?

May 31

"And it came to pass that while they were thus conversing one with another, they heard a voice as if it came out of heaven; ... and it was not a harsh voice, neither was it a loud voice; ... yea, it did pierce them to the very soul, and did cause their hearts to burn."

3 Nephi 11:3

The voice of the Lord is not loud or harsh. It is personal. It speaks spirit to spirit, reaching the deepest part of us. Sometimes it takes stillness to hear. Sometimes it takes practice. But always, it takes faith.

The people in the Book of Mormon heard the voice of God only after listening carefully and turning their hearts. The voice did not shout over the noise. It waited to be received.

One youth said she realized she was asking for answers but not making time to hear them. She started spending five minutes each night just listening after prayer. "I began to feel more clarity and more connection," she said.

God's voice comes in stillness. And when it does, it pierces the soul with truth and love.

Today, make time to listen. Not just to speak, but to receive. Let the voice of the Lord speak to your soul.

What small step can you take to make hearing Him a more intentional part of your day?

June

Trust in God's perfect timing with patience, enduring faith, and a heart willing to wait on Him.

June 1

> *"But if we hope for that we see not,* then *do we with patience wait for* it.*"*
>
> Romans 8:25

PATIENCE IS NOT PASSIVE. It is faithful waiting. It is the kind of hope that keeps showing up, even when there is no timeline and no clear outcome. Waiting with God is not wasted time. It is sacred preparation.

Sometimes we ask for answers and feel like heaven is silent. But the silence may be a space for growth. God is never absent. He is always working, even when we do not see it yet.

One woman prayed for healing she did not understand. Every day she waited felt long. But over time, she saw how the waiting changed her. "I stopped asking when it would be over," she said. "I started asking what I could learn while I waited."

Faith is not only believing in what God can do. It is trusting Him enough to wait on His perfect timing.

Today, ask the Lord how you can grow in the waiting. Trust that He is doing more than you can see.

What has the Lord already taught you through a season of waiting?

June 2

> *"For ye have need of patience, that, after ye have done the will of God, ye might receive the promise."*
>
> Hebrews 10:36

We often expect blessings to come quickly, especially when we are trying to be obedient. But scripture teaches us that patience is part of the promise. It shapes our faith. It refines our hearts. It prepares us to receive what God has planned.

God does not delay blessings to punish us. He prepares blessings to fit us. When the timing feels long, it is often because He is doing something deep, not just something fast.

A young man said he fasted and prayed for answers about his future but felt no clear direction. Months later, during a quiet walk, the answer came with peace. "I realized I needed the time in between," he said. "That space grew my trust."

God's promises are sure. So is His timing.

Today, thank the Lord for what He is doing in the in-between. Trust that His delay has purpose.

Where in your life is the Lord inviting you to be patient and trust the promise?

June 3

> *"... that all these things shall give thee experience, and shall be for thy good."*
> Doctrine and Covenants 122:7

There is something powerful about looking back and realizing that the hardest things shaped you the most. Trials rarely come with explanation, but they often come with eventual clarity. God uses experiences, not just ease, to prepare His children.

It does not mean every hard thing was sent by Him. But it does mean He can use every hard thing for your good. His timing is about eternity, not just the present moment.

One woman reflected on a season of long-suffering. "At the time, I thought I was just surviving," she said. "But now I see how deeply I was being strengthened. God was not in a hurry, but He was always near."

Trust in His process brings peace in the waiting.

Today, look at one past challenge and ask the Lord what good He brought from it. Let that perspective bring faith to what you face now.

How has the Lord turned your hardest experiences into spiritual growth?

June 4

> *"Behold, the Lord requireth the heart and a willing mind; ..."*
>
> Doctrine and Covenants 64:34

Sometimes we try to offer God results. We want to hand Him a finished product, a solved problem, a polished self. But what He asks for is much simpler and more sacred. He asks for a willing heart.

When answers do not come quickly, and when efforts feel unseen, the Lord is still watching. He sees the quiet trying. He sees the faithful waiting. He sees the willingness, even when there is not yet success.

One mother said she felt discouraged that her spiritual progress seemed so slow. "I was trying to do everything right, but I just felt stuck," she said. "Then the Spirit whispered, 'God sees your willing heart. That is enough for today.'"

Faith does not always feel like moving forward. Sometimes it feels like standing still with trust.

Today, offer the Lord your willing heart. Even if the answers are not clear, He knows your desire to follow Him.

What does a willing heart look like for you right now?

June 5

"(For we walk by faith, not by sight:)"
2 Corinthians 5:7

There are moments in every journey where the road ahead feels hidden. Plans change. Questions arise. Prayers seem to echo. And in those moments, the invitation remains the same, *walk by faith*.

Faith is not blindness. It is trust. It is choosing to move forward even when the outcome is uncertain. It is believing that God sees what we cannot and that He will guide us step by step.

One young adult shared how she faced an unexpected decision that felt overwhelming. "I wanted a perfect blueprint," she said. "Instead, God gave me peace for one step. That was enough."

When we walk with Christ, we do not need to see the whole map. We only need to follow His voice.

Today, take the next faithful step, even if the full path is unclear. Trust that God is already where you are going.

What is one step you can take in faith this week, even if the outcome is still unknown?

June 6

> "Nevertheless the Lord seeth fit to chasten his people; yea, he trieth their patience and their faith."
>
> Mosiah 23:21

Even the righteous experience trials. It is not always because of disobedience or weakness. Sometimes the Lord allows difficult experiences to deepen our patience and grow our faith. He is not testing to punish, but to prepare.

The people of Alma were faithful. Yet they were still led into bondage. And still, they trusted. Their deliverance did not come instantly, but it came. And in the waiting, they learned that God was aware of them all along.

One father said he had been praying for help with a long-standing challenge in his family. "I used to think God was silent," he said. "Now I believe He was teaching us how to rely on Him more fully."

God's delays are not denials. They are often His way of preparing us for something greater than we had imagined. While we may see delay as disappointment, He sees it as development. In the waiting, He is shaping us, refining our desires, and building the strength we will need for what is coming next.

Today, let your trial be a teacher. Ask the Lord what He is helping you become through it.

How has a season of testing helped strengthen your patience and faith?

June 7

> *"But let patience have her perfect work, that ye may be perfect and entire, wanting nothing."*
> James 1:4

Patience is not just waiting. It is becoming. When we choose to be patient, we are not simply enduring time, we are allowing the Lord to shape us through it. It is in that shaping that we grow in grace, humility, and depth.

Spiritual maturity often develops quietly. There may not be grand signs of progress, but each faithful choice builds something eternal. Each moment of patience adds to the soul.

A missionary once shared that the first months of her service felt slow and discouraging. "I thought I wasn't doing enough," she said. "But then I realized the Lord was doing something in me. He was teaching me to trust without seeing results."

When you let patience do its work, you invite the Savior to do His.

Today, trust that what feels slow may be exactly what God is using to help you grow. Let patience shape your soul.

How can you see your current waiting as part of God's refining process?

June 8

> *"For I the Lord thy God will hold thy right hand, saying unto thee, Fear not; I will help thee."*
>
> Isaiah 41:13

God's promises are not just distant hopes. They are present reassurances. When life feels uncertain or overwhelming, He is not far away. He is beside you, holding your hand, steadying your steps.

There is something deeply comforting about the image of the Savior walking with us; not rushing us, not pushing us, just staying near. His timing is often slower than ours, but it is always more perfect.

One woman said that when her prayers seemed unanswered, she started picturing Christ holding her hand through the day. "It didn't solve everything," she said, "but it changed everything. I no longer felt alone."

Patience becomes easier when you remember who is walking with you.

Today, picture Christ beside you. Let that image bring peace as you wait on His timing.

What helps you remember that the Lord is walking with you right now?

June 9

> *"Be still, and know that I am God: ..."*
> Psalm 46:10

Stillness is not the absence of struggle. It is the presence of trust. When everything feels loud, including your fears, your questions, and your to-do list, the invitation to "be still" is a call to remember who is in charge.

God is not rushed. He is not anxious. And when we anchor ourselves in Him, we do not have to be either. Stillness lets the Spirit speak. It helps us step out of panic and into peace.

A young adult said that in a season of stress, she began practicing one minute of silence after her morning prayers. "It didn't fix everything," she said, "but it reminded me that God was already present. That helped me start the day with more calm and more trust."

Stillness is not wasted time. It is space for God to remind us that He is near. In the quiet, we begin to feel His presence more clearly and trust that He is already at work in ways we cannot yet see.

Today, take a moment of stillness and let your spirit be quiet with God. Listen for His peace.

How can stillness help you trust God more fully in this season?

June 10

> *"And now I would that ye should be humble, and be submissive and gentle; easy to be entreated; full of patience and long-suffering; being temperate in all things; being diligent in keeping the commandments of God at all times; asking for whatsoever things ye stand in need, both spiritual and temporal; always returning thanks unto God for whatsoever things ye do receive."*
>
> Alma 7:23

Patience and long-suffering are not just traits we develop. They are spiritual gifts the Lord helps us cultivate as we let Him in. They soften our hearts, steady our pace, and help us endure well.

To be patient is not to give up. To be long-suffering is not to suffer endlessly, but to suffer with hope, believing that the Lord sees, strengthens, and sustains.

One sister said she learned the difference between enduring and enduring well when she began praying for strength instead of escape. "I asked the Lord to teach me, not just rescue me. That changed everything," she said.

God honors the strength it takes to keep going.

Today, ask the Lord to help you endure with faith. Let Him teach you what He needs you to learn.

How can you turn your current trial into an opportunity to grow in patience?

June 11

> *"And not only so, but we glory in tribulations also: knowing that tribulation worketh patience;"*
>
> Romans 5:3

It feels unnatural to see tribulation as something to glory in. But Paul reminds us that trials are not just obstacles, they are opportunities. They work something in us that comfort alone cannot.

Patience is shaped in adversity. It grows when we keep trusting, even when the outcome is unclear. And in that process, something changes. Our hearts expand. Our faith deepens. Our focus shifts from just wanting relief to wanting refinement.

One brother shared that during a long illness, he learned more about the Savior's empathy than he ever had before. "I didn't just pray for healing," he said. "I prayed to understand His grace. And I found it."

The path of patience leads to a deeper relationship with Christ.

Today, ask what your trial is teaching you, not just what it is taking from you. Let patience shape your perspective.

What has tribulation taught you about Christ that you may not have learned another way?

June 12

> "Trust in the Lord with all thine heart; and lean not unto thine own understanding. In all thy ways acknowledge him, and he shall direct thy paths. Be not wise in thine own eyes: fear the Lord, and depart from evil."
>
> Proverbs 3:5–7

There is a kind of peace that comes when we stop trying to figure everything out on our own. Trusting the Lord does not mean we have all the answers. It means we believe He does.

Our understanding is limited. His is eternal. And when we acknowledge Him in our plans, our pain, and our progression, He gently directs us, even when the path looks different than we expected.

One woman said she used to pray for clarity, but found more peace when she started praying for trust. "Answers came later," she said. "But the calm came right away."

Trust is not passive. It is a choice to believe that God is good, even when the timeline is not.

Today, choose to trust even if you do not yet understand. Let faith guide your next step.

Where in your life do you need to stop leaning on your own understanding and start leaning on Him?

June 13

> *"For ye have need of patience, that, after ye have done the will of God, ye might receive the promise."*
>
> Hebrews 10:36

Sometimes the hardest part of faith is the waiting that follows obedience. You do what the Lord asks. You give your best. And then you wait, often longer than expected, for the promised blessings to unfold.

This is the refining ground of discipleship. When answers are delayed or prayers feel unanswered, the Lord is still working. He honors every act of obedience, even when the results are not immediate.

One young man said he struggled when his efforts to serve others went unnoticed. "I wondered if it even mattered," he said. "But then I realized I wasn't waiting for approval. I was waiting for God's promise, and He always keeps His word."

Patience is not just about time. It is about trust in the One who holds time.

Today, remember that God sees every effort. Keep doing His will and trust that His promises will come.

What promise are you still waiting for? How can patience help you hold on a little longer?

June 14

> *"Nevertheless they did fast and pray oft, and did wax stronger and stronger in their humility, and firmer and firmer in the faith of Christ, unto the filling their souls with joy and consolation, yea, even to the purifying and the sanctification of their hearts, ..."*
>
> Helaman 3:35

Spiritual strength is not built in a moment. It is formed in the quiet consistency of discipleship, through repeated prayer, faithful fasting, and a heart that turns to Christ again and again.

When life feels slow or stagnant, it can be tempting to wonder if our spiritual efforts are making a difference. But like roots growing beneath the surface, faith grows strong in unseen ways.

One sister said she felt discouraged when answers didn't come right away. "But I kept showing up to pray and study," she said. "Months later, I realized I wasn't just waiting. I was being strengthened."

The Lord honors every effort to stay close to Him. And over time, those efforts shape a faith that is unshakable.

Today, keep doing the small things that draw you to Christ. Trust that your strength is growing.

What small spiritual habit can you keep or begin that will help you grow stronger in faith?

June 15

"But they that wait upon the Lord shall renew their strength; they shall mount up with wings as eagles; they shall run, and not be weary; and they shall walk, and not faint."

Isaiah 40:31

Waiting on the Lord is not idle. It is not doing nothing. It is trusting that something sacred is happening, even when it is not visible yet. In that waiting, God is not just preparing blessings. He is preparing you.

Strength does not always come before the trial. Often, it comes in the middle of it. As we wait with faith, the Lord renews our courage, steadies our heart, and helps us rise again.

One young adult shared that during a long season of unanswered prayers, she began to feel worn down. "But each time I prayed, I felt just enough peace to keep going," she said. "That was the strength I needed."

The Lord will always give you what you need to endure, even if He has not yet given what you asked for.

Today, ask the Lord for renewed strength, not just to wait, but to wait faithfully.

What strength has the Lord already given you to help you keep going?

June 16

> *"Know ye not that ye are in the hands of God? Know ye not that he hath all power, and at his great command the earth shall be rolled together as a scroll?"*
>
> Mormon 5:23

There are moments when patience feels like silence and long-suffering feels like being forgotten. But the truth is, you are never out of God's sight. He does not overlook His children. He remembers you. Your prayers, your efforts, your hopes.

He may not answer on your timeline, but He always answers. Sometimes the waiting is not because He has turned away, but because He is working in ways you do not yet see.

One woman said that after years of praying for something dear to her heart, she finally received an answer. "It wasn't the answer I expected," she said, "but it reminded me that God had been listening the whole time."

You are not cast off. You are deeply remembered.

Today, hold onto the truth that the Lord is aware of you. Let that reminder bring peace to your waiting.

When have you felt remembered by the Lord in a quiet or unexpected way?

June 17

> *"For we through the Spirit wait for the hope of righteousness by faith."*
>
> Galatians 5:5

Waiting is not always easy, but it is always meaningful when we wait with the Spirit. Through Him, our hope is sustained. Our faith is strengthened. And our vision begins to shift from what we lack to what we are becoming.

The Spirit does not just help us endure. He helps us endure with grace. When we invite Him into the waiting, we begin to feel peace even before the answers come. We find joy in trusting that God is at work.

One young man said he learned to rely on the Spirit during a time of uncertainty about his future. "I didn't get instant direction," he said. "But I felt calm. That was enough to keep me moving forward with faith."

When you wait with the Spirit, you are never waiting alone.

Today, invite the Holy Ghost into your waiting. Let His peace give you strength and hope.

How has the Spirit helped you wait in faith, even when the future was unclear?

June 18

> *"That ye be not slothful, but followers of them who through faith and patience inherit the promises."*
>
> Hebrews 6:12

The promises of God are sure, but they often unfold slowly. They come to those who follow with faith and wait with patience. That combination of faith in what is unseen and patience in what is delayed leads to spiritual inheritance.

Following Christ is not about rushing to the reward. It is about trusting in the process, knowing that every step matters. Even when results are not immediate, the Lord is always moving His work forward, including the work He is doing in you.

One woman shared that she kept a list of promises from her patriarchal blessing and reviewed them during her scripture study. "It helped me stay focused," she said. "I realized I was still on the path, even if I hadn't arrived yet."

Faith keeps you moving. Patience keeps you grounded.

Today, reflect on a promise God has made to you. Trust that He is preparing to fulfill it in His time.

What helps you stay faithful when the fulfillment of a promise feels far away?

June 19

> *"And blessed are all they who do hunger and thirst after righteousness, for they shall be filled with the Holy Ghost."*
>
> 3 Nephi 12:6

Spiritual hunger is a sign of faith. When we long for righteousness, when we desire to be filled with truth and peace, the Lord promises to respond. But that filling does not always come instantly. It comes with time, with seeking, and with patience.

Just as a seed does not grow overnight, spiritual fulfillment takes nurturing. The Holy Ghost fills us gradually as we return to the Lord again and again in prayer, study, and quiet devotion.

One sister shared that during a season of spiritual drought, she kept returning to her scriptures each day, even when she felt nothing. "Then one day, the words felt alive again," she said. "It came quietly, but it came."

Those who hunger for righteousness will be filled. That is a promise the Lord keeps.

Today, ask the Lord to fill you with His Spirit. Keep seeking, trusting that He will answer your hunger.

What do you spiritually hunger for right now? How can you keep coming to Christ to receive it?

June 20

> *"And I will also ease the burdens which are put upon your shoulders, that even you cannot feel them upon your backs, even while you are in bondage; and this will I do that ye may stand as witnesses for me hereafter, and that ye may know of a surety that I, the Lord God, do visit my people in their afflictions."*
>
> Mosiah 24:14

Sometimes we pray for our burdens to be taken away, but the Lord answers by strengthening our backs instead. He may not always remove the trial, but He will always help us carry it. His promise is not just relief. It is support.

The people of Alma were not immediately delivered from bondage, but their burdens were made light. They felt peace in the middle of struggle. That is one of the quiet miracles of patience and faith.

One father shared how a heavy season of responsibility did not end quickly, but he found unexpected strength. "The problems didn't vanish," he said. "But I felt carried in a way I could not explain."

God's help often comes in quiet ways that lift what we thought we could not bear.

Today, ask the Lord not only to ease your burdens but to strengthen you to carry them.

When have you felt the Lord lighten your load even when the trial remained?

June 21

> *"And now it came to pass that the burdens which were laid upon Alma and his brethren were made light; yea, the Lord did strengthen them that they could bear up their burdens with ease, and they did submit cheerfully and with patience to all the will of the Lord."*
>
> Mosiah 24:15

There is beauty in the way the Lord strengthens His people. He does not always change the circumstance, but He changes the heart within it. His strength comes quietly, helping us bear up rather than break down.

Faith does not eliminate hardship. It transforms it. With the Lord, even burdens become bearable. His timing may not align with our hopes, but His strength always arrives when it is most needed.

One woman shared that during a time of uncertainty, she prayed for direction but found peace instead. "I didn't get clarity," she said, "but I felt calm. That was how the Lord strengthened me."

Strength to endure is one of the tender mercies of waiting in faith.

Today, thank the Lord for the strength He gives you in your burdens. Ask Him to help you recognize it more clearly.

When has the Lord's quiet strength helped you endure more than you thought you could?

June 22

> *"And now, behold, my beloved brethren, this is the way; and there is none other way nor name given under heaven whereby man can be saved in the kingdom of God. And now, behold, this is the doctrine of Christ, and the only and true doctrine of the Father, and of the Son, and of the Holy Ghost, which is one God, without end. Amen."*
>
> 2 Nephi 31:21

Trusting the Lord's timing also means trusting His way. His path may not always be fast or easy, but it is always right. It leads to peace, even when the steps feel slow.

The Savior's way is marked by patience, mercy, and endurance. He does not ask us to run faster than we have strength. He simply asks us to walk with Him, one faithful step at a time.

One young adult shared that her plans kept falling apart. "Nothing went the way I expected," she said. "But as I looked back, I could see that every change was gently guiding me toward something better."

There is no better path than the one that keeps you close to Christ.

Today, choose His way over your own. Trust that He sees the full picture even when you do not.

Where might the Lord be inviting you to follow a slower, but holier, path?

June 23

> *"Therefore, let your hearts be comforted; for all things shall work together for good to them that walk uprightly, and to the sanctification of the church."*
> Doctrine and Covenants 100:15

God's promises are rarely about ease. They are about eventual good. When we walk uprightly, even our disappointments and delays are gathered into something meaningful. Nothing is wasted in His hands.

We may not see how it all fits right now, but the Lord is a Master Weaver. He turns broken pieces into purpose. He brings beauty from waiting and wisdom from struggle.

One brother said he used to resent unanswered prayers. "Now I see that some of the greatest blessings in my life came from things I did not plan," he said. "God saw the whole picture. I only saw a corner."

When you walk with God, everything has purpose. Even the hard parts.

Today, take comfort that God is working all things together for your good. Keep walking with Him.

How has the Lord used something unexpected in your life to lead you somewhere better?

June 24

> *"For after much tribulation come the blessings. Wherefore the day cometh that ye shall be crowned with much glory; the hour is not yet, but is nigh at hand."*
> Doctrine and Covenants 58:4

Blessings do not always come when we want them. Sometimes they come after the wrestle, after the waiting, after the tears. But they do come. The Lord is not slow. He is deliberate. He gives us what will bless us most, when we are ready to receive it.

Tribulation stretches our faith. It refines our character. It prepares us to recognize and value the blessings when they finally arrive.

One woman shared that she waited many years for a prayer to be answered. When it came, it felt more personal and powerful than she had imagined. "The waiting changed me," she said. "It made the blessing even sweeter."

With God, no tribulation is wasted. It is always leading toward something holy.

Today, remember that every trial has an ending, and every faithful journey leads to blessing.

What blessing are you still waiting for? How can you let hope grow even in the waiting?

June 25

"In your patience possess ye your souls."
Luke 21:19

Patience is more than just waiting. It is a way of keeping your soul anchored when life feels unsteady. Through patience, you learn to hold peace, to choose calm, and to trust deeply in the timing of the Lord.

This kind of patience does not come all at once. It comes through small, repeated choices to stay close to Christ, even when things do not make sense. It grows when you surrender control and rest in His wisdom.

One young woman shared that during a difficult trial, she wrote the word "patience" on a card and carried it in her pocket. "Every time I touched it, I remembered that my soul was safe in Christ," she said.

Patience keeps the soul steady when everything else is shifting.

Today, choose one way to slow down and trust God. Let patience hold your heart steady.

What helps you stay anchored in Christ when life feels uncertain?

June 26

> *"For my thoughts are not your thoughts, neither are your ways my ways, saith the Lord."*
>
> Isaiah 55:8

Trusting God's timing means trusting that His perspective is greater than ours. What we see as delay, He may see as preparation. What we view as unanswered, He may be answering in ways we cannot yet understand.

God sees the whole story. He knows the beginning, the middle, and the end. While we might only see a single chapter, He is already working on the outcome. His ways are higher, and His timing is always rooted in love.

One young man said he had plans that kept falling through, and it left him frustrated. Later, he realized that every closed door had gently redirected him to something better. "I didn't see it then," he said, "but now I see the Lord's hand in every detail."

When you cannot see the full plan, trust the One who made it.

Today, release the need to understand everything right now. Choose to trust the wisdom of God's ways.

When has the Lord's higher way led you somewhere you did not expect, but needed to go?

June 27

> *"Wait on the Lord: be of good courage, and he shall strengthen thine heart: wait, I say, on the Lord."*
>
> Psalm 27:14

Waiting is not weakness. It is an act of courage. It means trusting the Lord enough to stay where you are until He tells you to move. It means believing that His promises are worth the time they take.

The heart grows strong in waiting when it is centered on Christ. He does not ask you to wait alone. He stands beside you, strengthening your soul with quiet reassurance, with tender mercies, and with the peace of His presence.

One woman said she began reading this verse every day during a long season of uncertainty. "It became my promise," she said. "I was not just waiting. I was being strengthened."

Waiting with Christ builds a strength the world cannot give.

Today, choose courage in your waiting. Ask the Lord to strengthen your heart and remind you of His promises.

How has God strengthened your heart when you chose to wait with courage?

June 28

> "The Lord is not slack concerning his promise, as some men count slackness; but is longsuffering to us-ward, not willing that any should perish, but that all should come to repentance."
>
> 2 Peter 3:9

Sometimes it feels like the promises of God are slow to come. But the Lord is never late. He is intentional. He works with perfect timing, not rushed by our impatience or limited by our expectations.

What seems like delay may actually be preparation. While we are waiting, the Lord is arranging, refining, and readying us to receive what He intends to give.

One brother shared that a dream he had prayed about for years was finally fulfilled. "When it came, I saw why it had taken so long," he said. "God had been shaping me so I could receive it the right way."

The Lord never forgets His promises. He fulfills them when the time is right and when your heart is ready.

Today, trust that God has not forgotten what He has promised you. Hold on with hope.

What has God promised that you are still holding onto? How can you show faith while you wait?

June 29

> *"Behold my Spirit is upon you, wherefore all thy words will I justify; and the mountains shall flee before you, and the rivers shall turn from their course; and thou shalt abide in me, and I in you; therefore walk with me."*
>
> Moses 6:34

To trust God's timing is also to trust His companionship. He does not ask you to wait alone or walk uncertain paths by yourself. He invites you to walk with Him—to abide in Him—and to find peace in His presence even when the path is unclear.

Walking with Christ means choosing faith in every season, not just the easy ones. It means believing He is close, even when heaven feels quiet. The promise is not that you will always understand, but that you will never be alone.

One young woman said she began saying the words "Walk with me, Lord" at the start of each day. "It reminded me I was not carrying anything by myself," she said. "He was right there, every step."

You do not have to see the full path. You just need to walk it with the Savior.

Today, invite Christ to walk with you. Let His nearness calm your heart and steady your steps.

How do you feel His presence more clearly when you choose to walk with Him?

June 30

> "Therefore, he giveth this promise unto you, with an immutable covenant that they shall be fulfilled; and all things wherewith you have been afflicted shall work together for your good, and to my name's glory, saith the Lord."
>
> Doctrine and Covenants 98:3

God does not waste anything. Not your pain, not your delays, not your waiting. Every affliction has the potential to become part of a greater purpose when placed in His hands. He turns sorrow into growth and waiting into preparation.

When you trust His timing, you begin to see trials not just as obstacles, but as sacred tools. He is shaping something in you that is meant to last. Even if you cannot yet see the full picture, He is working all things for your good.

One missionary said she did not understand why her first area was so hard. "But when I got to my next assignment, I realized I had been prepared in ways I never expected," she said. "God used everything to help me serve better."

He is using everything to help you become who He knows you can be.

Today, thank the Lord for how He is shaping your journey. Trust that every step has purpose.

How have you seen afflictions work for your good in ways you did not expect?

July

Live your covenants with purpose, drawing strength from sacred ordinances, temple worship, and the promises of the Lord.

July 1

> *"Therefore, hold up your light that it may shine unto the world. Behold I am the light which ye shall hold up—that which ye have seen me do. Behold ye see that I have prayed unto the Father, and ye all have witnessed."*
>
> 3 Nephi 18:24

To LIVE A COVENANT life is to walk in the light of Christ and to reflect that light to others. Through sacred ordinances, we make promises with God. Through daily discipleship, we keep those promises. The temple reminds us who we are. Our covenants remind us who we follow.

Covenants are not just about Sunday worship or temple attendance. They are about choosing Christ again and again. In our thoughts. In our actions. In the way we serve and love and repent.

One young man shared how, after receiving his endowment, he began to see his daily choices differently. "I started thinking more about who I was becoming," he said. "It wasn't about being perfect. It was about being loyal to Christ."

Covenants are not burdens. They are anchors that keep us steady in a shifting world.

Today, reflect on the covenants you have made. Ask the Lord how you can live them more fully.

How has making and keeping covenants strengthened your relationship with Jesus Christ?

July 2

> *"Yea, he saith: Come unto me and ye shall partake of the fruit of the tree of life; yea, ye shall eat and drink of the bread and the waters of life freely;"*
>
> Alma 5:34

The Savior's invitation is personal and ongoing. He calls us to come, to partake, and to become. Through our covenants, we respond to that call continually.

Covenants are not a demand for flawlessness. They are a divine invitation to draw near to Christ and receive of His goodness. He offers us the bread and waters of life freely. As we bring forth works of righteousness, we grow in our ability to reflect His light and live His gospel more fully.

One woman said that renewing her covenants each Sunday helped her realign with the Savior. "It felt like I was being nourished spiritually. That weekly recommitment gave me strength to keep going with Him."

Covenants connect us to Christ's grace and keep us rooted in His love.

Today, reflect on how your covenants are helping you answer the Savior's invitation to come unto Him.

What helps you bring forth works of righteousness as a response to His call?

July 3

> *"Know ye not that ye are the temple of God, and that the Spirit of God dwelleth in you?"*
> 1 Corinthians 3:16

Covenant living begins with identity. When we make sacred promises with God, we are reminded of who we are—His sons and daughters, set apart, filled with divine potential. We are not just invited to enter holy places. We are invited to become holy people.

The Spirit can dwell in a soul that is striving, not perfect. When we honor our covenants, we invite His presence more fully into our lives. That presence changes how we think, how we speak, and how we see ourselves and others.

One young adult said she began to treat herself with more kindness after a visit to the temple. "I felt something there that reminded me I was more than I had been acting like," she said. "I left knowing I wanted to live up to who I really am."

To live your covenants is to live in a way that reflects your divine worth.

Today, ask the Lord to help you see yourself as a covenant child of God. Let that truth shape your choices.

What changes when you remember that you are the temple of God?

July 4

> "I tell you these things because of your prayers; wherefore, treasure up wisdom in your bosoms, lest the wickedness of men reveal these things unto you by their wickedness, in a manner which shall speak in your ears with a voice louder than that which shall shake the earth; but if ye are prepared ye shall not fear."
>
> Doctrine and Covenants 38:30

Covenant living prepares us spiritually for whatever lies ahead. The world offers uncertainty, but the gospel offers promises. Through covenants, we align ourselves with the power of God, and that alignment brings peace. Even in the face of difficulty.

Preparation is more than storage and plans. It is about being spiritually steady. When we keep our covenants, we are spiritually grounded. We are ready to respond with faith instead of fear, with confidence instead of confusion.

One young man said he felt peace going into a season of unknowns because of a recent temple visit. "I didn't leave with all the answers," he said. "But I left with clarity about who I belong to. That gave me strength."

Covenants prepare us by connecting us to Christ.

Today, consider how your covenants have prepared you to face the unknown with faith.

How does covenant keeping help you feel more secure in an uncertain world?

July 5

> *"... I will go and do the things which the Lord hath commanded, for I know that the Lord giveth no commandments unto the children of men, save he shall prepare a way for them that they may accomplish the thing which he commandeth them."*
>
> 1 Nephi 3:7

Covenants are not just promises we make, they are commitments we act on. They shape the way we respond to the Lord's commandments, even when those commandments feel challenging or unclear.

Nephi's words reflect the heart of a covenant disciple. He trusted that if the Lord asked, He would also provide a way. That trust is what made Nephi's obedience possible, and it is what can make ours steady and consistent.

One sister shared that after receiving her endowment, she began asking in her prayers, "What would Thou have me do today?" She said, "It wasn't always something big. But it helped me live with more purpose and more peace."

Living our covenants means being willing to act, not just believe.

Today, ask the Lord what He would have you do as part of your covenant path. Then take one small step in faith.

What helps you act with more faith when the Lord gives you a commandment or direction?

July 6

> *"Therefore, in the ordinances thereof, the power of godliness is manifest."*
> Doctrine and Covenants 84:20

God's power is not just something we read about in scripture. It is something we can experience. Ordinances are sacred moments where heaven touches earth. They are more than rituals. They are real connections with divine power.

Every ordinance we receive, from baptism to the sacrament to temple covenants, brings us closer to God and invites His strength into our lives. That strength is what carries us through trials, refines our character, and helps us become more like Him.

One young adult said she didn't fully understand the temple the first time she went, but she felt something she couldn't explain. "I left knowing I was part of something eternal," she said. "And I wanted to return."

Ordinances do not just remind us of God's power. They help us receive it.

Today, reflect on the last ordinance you received. What power did it bring into your life?

How can you prepare more intentionally for the ordinances you participate in?

July 7

"Wherefore, stand ye in holy places, and be not moved, until the day of the Lord come; for behold, it cometh quickly, saith the Lord. Amen."

Doctrine and Covenants 87:8

Covenant living calls us to seek holiness, not only in places but also in our hearts. When we choose to stand in holy places, whether in temples, homes, or moments of personal devotion, we invite spiritual strength. And when we choose to be not moved, we commit to staying true to our covenants no matter the pressure around us.

Holiness is not limited to sacred buildings. It is cultivated in quiet decisions, in reverent choices, in moments where we choose Christ again.

One brother shared that when he could not attend the temple for a season, he created a "holy place" at home. "I made a quiet spot for study and prayer," he said. "It reminded me that holiness is something we carry with us."

Your covenants can make any place a holy place when you stand in them with faith.

Today, create space for holiness in your life. Stand firm in your covenants, no matter your surroundings.

What helps you stand in holy places when life feels unsettled or uncertain?

July 8

> *"I, the Lord, am bound when ye do what I say; but when ye do not what I say, ye have no promise."*
>
> Doctrine and Covenants 82:10

God keeps His promises. Always. Covenants are sacred agreements where we bind ourselves to Him, and He binds Himself to us. He never fails on His end. His power and blessings are sure, but they are also conditional on our willingness to obey.

That truth is not meant to scare us. It is meant to encourage us. When we keep our covenants, we invite the full strength of heaven into our lives.

One woman shared that during a time of financial uncertainty, she and her husband continued to pay tithing. "We had no idea how things would work out," she said. "But we kept our covenant, and somehow, the Lord provided every time."

Covenants open the door to divine help. And God's promises never expire.

Today, reflect on a time when God fulfilled a promise in your life. Let that memory strengthen your faith.

How can keeping your covenants help you trust more fully in God's promises?

July 9

"Who shall ascend into the hill of the Lord? or who shall stand in his holy place? He that hath clean hands, and a pure heart; who hath not lifted up his soul unto vanity, nor sworn deceitfully."

Psalm 24:3–4

Temple worship invites us into the presence of the Lord. It is not about earning access. It is about preparing ourselves to receive what He wants to give. Clean hands and a pure heart are not signs of perfection. They are signs of sincere effort and humility.

The temple is a place of revelation, renewal, and remembrance. We go not because we are flawless, but because we are faithful.

One young man said he felt nervous before his first temple trip. "I worried I wouldn't feel worthy," he said. "But I felt welcomed. I left with a deeper desire to be better, not out of fear but out of love for the Lord."

The temple is not just a place we visit. It is a pattern we bring into our lives.

Today, recommit to preparing your heart for temple worship. Let that preparation become part of your everyday discipleship.

What helps you feel more ready to enter the Lord's house and stand in holy places?

July 10

> *"And they entered into a covenant to seek the Lord God of their fathers with all their heart and with all their soul."*
>
> 2 Chronicles 15:12

Covenants are about wholehearted discipleship. They are not half-promises or occasional commitments. They invite us to seek the Lord with everything we are and everything we hope to become.

When we enter into covenants, we offer our hearts. And in return, the Lord offers His strength, His peace, and His transforming grace. The more we give, the more we receive.

One woman said that after renewing her temple recommend, she started reading her patriarchal blessing more often. "It reminded me of what I promised and what God has promised me. That connection gave me spiritual momentum."

Covenants keep our hearts turned toward heaven, even in the middle of everyday life.

Today, reflect on what it means to seek the Lord with your whole heart. Let that guide your intentions.

What does wholehearted covenant living look like in your life right now?

July 11

"And if men come unto me I will show unto them their weakness. I give unto men weakness that they may be humble; and my grace is sufficient for all men that humble themselves before me; for if they humble themselves before me, and have faith in me, then will I make weak things become strong unto them."

Ether 12:27

Covenant living does not require perfection. It requires humility. As we come unto Christ through sacred covenants, He reveals our weaknesses not to shame us, but to help us grow. He meets us where we are and gently invites us to become more.

Every time we fall short, He invites us back. Every time we return, He offers grace. Our covenants remind us that progress is possible because of His mercy and strength.

One brother said he used to feel discouraged by his weaknesses. "But now I see them as invitations," he said. "Each one is a chance to rely more fully on Christ."

Weakness is not the end of the covenant path. It is often the very place where Christ begins His greatest work.

Today, bring your weakness to the Lord. Let Him turn it into strength through your covenant relationship with Him.

What has the Lord taught you about grace through your personal imperfections?

July 12

> *"And this is life eternal, that they might know thee the only true God, and Jesus Christ, whom thou hast sent."*
>
> John 17:3

Covenants deepen our relationship with God. They are not just commitments to follow rules. They are sacred invitations to come to know Him. As we keep our covenants, we do not just become more obedient. We become more acquainted with the heart of the Savior.

Knowing Christ means walking with Him. It means remembering Him at the sacrament table, seeking Him in the temple, and inviting Him into our daily lives. That kind of knowledge is not academic. It is relational and transformational.

One woman said she felt her connection to Christ grow as she began praying more intentionally after taking the sacrament. "It became personal," she said. "I wasn't just remembering a Savior. I was talking to my Savior."

Covenants are the bridge between knowing about Christ and truly knowing Him.

Today, seek to know Christ more personally through the covenants you have made.

What helps you feel more connected to Christ as you walk the covenant path?

July 13

"And know ye that ye shall be judges of this people, according to the judgment which I shall give unto you, which shall be just. Therefore, what manner of men ought ye to be? Verily I say unto you, even as I am."
3 Nephi 27:27

Covenant living is about becoming. It is about shaping our lives after the example of Jesus Christ. When we make covenants, we commit to becoming more like Him. Not instantly. Not perfectly. But steadily and sincerely.

Becoming like Christ is not about checking spiritual boxes. It is about changing our nature through grace and consistent discipleship. Each time we forgive, serve, repent, or love more deeply, we are living our covenants.

One young adult said she started asking herself this question each morning: "What would a disciple of Christ do today?" She said, "It helped me show up differently. Not to impress anyone, but to be more like Him."

Covenants are not just promises. They are a path to transformation.

Today, choose one Christlike attribute to focus on. Let your covenants help you live it more fully.

What attribute of Christ do you feel inspired to develop as part of your covenant journey?

July 14

> *"Behold, I have graven thee upon the palms of my hands; thy walls are continually before me."*
>
> Isaiah 49:16

Covenants are a reflection of how deeply the Savior loves us. He has not forgotten you. He remembers you with perfect clarity, with enduring mercy, and with marks of sacrifice that are eternal.

When you make and keep covenants, you are not just promising to remember Him. You are responding to the reality that He has always remembered you. He bore your name, your burdens, and your hopes long before you made any promise at all.

One young man said he often felt unworthy to renew his covenants. But one Sunday during the sacrament, he pictured the Savior holding out His hands. "I remembered He already gave everything for me," he said. "And all He asks is that I keep trying."

Covenants are not just about our commitment. They are about Christ's everlasting love.

Today, remember that you are already written on His hands. Let that truth anchor you in grace.

How does knowing Christ remembers you change how you remember Him?

July 15

> *"And now, because of the covenant which ye have made ye shall be called the children of Christ, his sons, and his daughters; for behold, this day he hath spiritually begotten you; for ye say that your hearts are changed through faith on his name; therefore, ye are born of him and have become his sons and his daughters."*
>
> Mosiah 5:7

Covenants give us a new identity. They are not just about behavior. They are about belonging. When we take upon ourselves the name of Christ, we accept a sacred role. We become part of His family and part of His work.

Being called a child of Christ means we walk differently. We forgive more easily, serve more willingly, and speak more kindly. Not because we are perfect, but because we remember whose name we carry.

One sister said that when she struggled with her self-worth, she would say quietly to herself, "I am a child of Christ." She said, "That one sentence changed the way I prayed and the way I lived."

Your covenants remind you who you are and whose you are.

Today, live like someone who belongs to Christ. Let that identity shape your thoughts and actions.

What does it mean to be called a child of Christ?

July 16

> *"Making and keeping covenants means choosing to bind ourselves to our Father in Heaven and Jesus Christ."*
> Sister Linda K. Burton

Covenants are sacred connections. They bind us to God in a relationship of trust, devotion, and love. When we choose to make covenants, we are not just committing to a lifestyle. We are committing to a divine partnership.

Binding ourselves to God does not mean we never stumble. It means that when we do, we return. It means we keep trying, keep trusting, and keep turning to Him who has already promised never to turn away.

One woman said that temple worship changed how she saw her relationship with God. "It was no longer about duty," she said. "It became about connection. I wasn't just following Him. I was walking with Him."

Covenants are not restrictions. They are relationships that lead us back to Him.

Today, reflect on what it means to be bound to the Savior. Ask Him to help you feel that connection more deeply.

How has making and keeping covenants helped you feel closer to God?

July 17

> *"And ye shall be my people, and I will be your God."*
>
> Jeremiah 30:22

This is the heart of every covenant. God invites us into a relationship that is both deeply personal and eternally powerful. When we promise to be His, He promises to be ours, not just in times of ease, but through every challenge and change.

Being the Lord's people means choosing to let Him lead, trusting His timing, and living in a way that reflects our commitment to Him. It means remembering who we belong to when the world pulls us in other directions.

One woman said that each time she entered the temple, she felt the Lord saying, "You are still mine." She said, "It gave me peace, even when I felt like I had fallen short. I just kept coming back."

Covenants are not just about what we promise. They are also about what God promises, to love us, guide us, and claim us as His own.

Today, take a moment to quietly reaffirm, "I am His." Let that identity shape your thoughts and your choices.

What helps you feel the security and belonging that come from being God's covenant child?

July 18

> *"And now, behold, I say unto you, that the thing which will be of the most worth unto you will be to declare repentance unto this people, that you may bring souls unto me, that you may rest with them in the kingdom of my Father. Amen."*
>
> Doctrine and Covenants 15:6

Covenant living is not only personal, it is outward-reaching. When we bind ourselves to Christ, we also commit to help others come to Him. Sharing the gospel, serving others, and inviting those around us to feel His love are natural expressions of our covenant path.

This does not always mean grand gestures. Often it is quiet, consistent kindness. It is living in a way that makes others feel the peace and light of the Savior through you.

One young woman said she began each day asking the Lord who she could serve. "It helped me remember that my covenants are not just about me. They're about helping others feel what I feel through Christ."

Our covenants connect us to God and call us to love one another.

Today, ask the Lord how you can help someone feel His love. Then follow the prompting.

How does your covenant relationship with Christ inspire you to reach outward and lift others?

July 19

"But I command you, all ye my saints, to build a house unto me; and I grant unto you a sufficient time to build a house unto me; and during this time your baptisms shall be acceptable unto me."

Doctrine and Covenants 124:31

The Lord sees our sacrifices. He knows the quiet efforts, the faithful choices, and the moments when we choose Him over convenience or comfort. Covenant living is made up of these daily offerings. simple, sincere, and seen by God.

Sometimes our offerings feel small. But when given with a willing heart, they are sacred. God does not measure worth by size. He measures by intent, by devotion, and by love.

One father shared that he tried to read scriptures with his children each night, even when they were tired or distracted. "It didn't always go well," he said. "But I trusted the Lord saw my effort. That made it holy."

Every time you choose Christ, no matter how quietly, it matters to Him.

Today, offer something to the Lord through your covenants; a moment of prayer, a quiet act of service, a faithful decision.

What small offering can you give today as a sign of your love for the Savior?

July 20

> *"... a covenant is a binding spiritual contract, a solemn promise to God our Father that we will live and think and act in a certain way—the way of His Son, the Lord Jesus Christ."*
>
> Elder Jeffrey R. Holland

Covenants are not casual. They are sacred commitments to live in alignment with the Savior's life and teachings. In this holy relationship, we promise to follow Him, and He promises to lead us toward eternal life.

The Lord sets the terms. We choose to accept them. That choice becomes a pattern of discipleship. It is expressed in the quiet decisions of daily life and reflected in the desires of our hearts.

One young adult said he began praying with the words of a hymn in mind: "I'll go where you want me to go. I'll be what you want me to be." He said, "It changed how I approached my decisions. I was no longer just asking for help. I was asking to be led."

Covenant living is about choosing the Lord's way again and again, until it becomes your way too.

Today, recommit to the sacred contract you have made with God. Let it guide your thoughts, choices, and desires.

How can you more fully live the way of the Savior through your covenants today?

July 21

"Teach them to never be weary of good works, but to be meek and lowly in heart; for such shall find rest to their souls."

Alma 37:34

Covenant living is about consistency. It is the quiet, daily choosing of good. It is doing what is right, even when it is repetitive, unnoticed, or difficult. And it is trusting that every good work matters to the Lord.

The world may not celebrate humility or perseverance, but God does. He strengthens those who stay the course, who keep serving, who keep praying, and who keep returning to Him in quiet devotion.

One sister said that for years she felt like her efforts at home and church were not making a difference. "But then one day, I realized how different my spirit felt. The Lord had been changing me through the good I kept choosing."

Your covenants are lived out in your actions. They grow stronger with every faithful step.

Today, do something good without needing recognition. Let it be your covenant offering to the Lord.

What helps you keep choosing good even when it feels ordinary or hard?

July 22

"Holiness to the Lord"
Inscription on every temple of The Church
of Jesus Christ of Latter-day Saints

Those four words are more than architecture. They are a reminder of our divine purpose. Holiness is not just something we visit in a building. It is something we strive to carry with us into our homes, our thoughts, and our daily choices.

Covenant living invites us to be holy. Not perfect, but devoted. It means we strive to reflect the purity and peace of the temple in how we live.

One woman shared how she started treating her home like a temple. "I prayed more, cleaned with purpose, and tried to make it a place of peace. It changed the spirit in our family."

Holiness is a habit of the heart. It grows in quiet, intentional living.

Today, choose one way to bring temple-like holiness into your surroundings. Let your covenants guide the atmosphere you create.

What helps you carry the spirit of the temple into your everyday life?

July 23

> *"Verily I say unto you, all among them who know their hearts are honest, and are broken, and their spirits contrite, and are willing to observe their covenants by sacrifice—yea, every sacrifice which I, the Lord, shall command—they are accepted of me."*
>
> Doctrine and Covenants 97:8

Covenant keeping is not about perfection. It is about willingness. The Lord asks for a broken heart and a contrite spirit, not flawless performance. When we offer ourselves in humility and faith, He accepts us.

Sacrifice is part of covenant living. Sometimes it means letting go of distractions or desires. Sometimes it means choosing what is right even when it is hard. But every sacrifice made with love draws us closer to the Savior.

One brother shared that when he gave up a personal goal to serve a mission, he did not feel loss. "I felt peace," he said. "It was my offering to the Lord, and He filled me with more than I gave up."

The Lord always honors the willing heart.

Today, offer a small sacrifice as a sign of your devotion. Let it remind you that you are accepted of Him.

> What does it mean to you to be accepted by the Lord, even when your offering feels small?

July 24

> *"And this was their faith, that by so doing God would prosper them in the land, or in other words, if they were faithful in keeping the commandments of God that he would prosper them in the land; ..."*
>
> Alma 48:15

Pioneer faith was built on covenant trust. Those early Saints gave everything for the Lord. Their sacrifices were not just about hardship. They were about commitment. They walked into the unknown because they believed in promises that would last forever.

Your covenant path may not look like theirs, but the heart of it is the same—obedience, sacrifice, and unwavering trust in Christ.

One woman said she felt closer to her pioneer ancestors when she made her own sacrifices for the gospel. "I realized I was walking the same kind of path. Different landscape, same faith."

You are part of the same covenant story. Your sacrifices matter just as much.

Today, honor the pioneers by walking your covenant path with renewed faith and quiet courage.

What can you learn from the example of early Saints as you keep your own sacred promises?

July 25

"Behold, I will lead thee by my hand, and I will take thee, to put upon thee my name, even the Priesthood of thy father, and my power shall be over thee."

Abraham 1:18

Covenants link us to eternal promises. They are not just about the present moment. They are about the future God is shaping for us and through us. When Abraham entered into a covenant with the Lord, he was promised blessings that extended beyond his lifetime. Those same blessings are available to us.

Every time we keep a covenant, we step into the story of those eternal promises. We become part of something greater than ourselves.

One young man said he started feeling more purpose when he remembered that his choices today affect generations. "Keeping my covenants helped me see I was building something bigger—something sacred."

Covenant living is about legacy. It connects us to promises that last forever.

Today, think about the future blessings your faithfulness is preparing. Let that give you purpose in the present.

How does remembering eternal promises change the way you live your covenants now?

July 26

> *"Teaching them to observe all things whatsoever I have commanded you: and, lo, I am with you alway, even unto the end of the world. Amen."*
>
> Matthew 28:20

The greatest blessing of covenant living is the companionship of Jesus Christ. He does not just give commandments and promises. He gives Himself. He walks with you. He strengthens you. He stays.

When you keep your covenants, you are not walking alone. The Lord is bound to you by His word and by His love. He will not leave you to figure it out by yourself.

One sister shared that during a very lonely season, she kept returning to the temple. "Every time I walked in, I felt Him walking with me," she said. "I was never truly alone."

Your covenants are a promise of His presence.

Today, invite the Savior into your covenant keeping. Let His presence bring peace and assurance.

When have you most clearly felt that the Lord was walking with you?

July 27

"Draw near unto me and I will draw near unto you; seek me diligently and ye shall find me; ask, and ye shall receive; knock, and it shall be opened unto you."
Doctrine and Covenants 88:63

Covenant living is about closeness with God. When we draw near to Him through our sacred promises, He responds with nearness, light, and personal revelation. He never forces connection. He invites it.

Every covenant you make is an invitation to draw closer. It is not about religious routine. It is about spiritual relationship. As we choose to come unto Christ, He meets us with mercy and walks with us through every part of life.

One young woman said she felt distant from God until she began preparing more intentionally for the sacrament. "That small shift changed everything," she said. "I felt Him closer, because I was coming closer."

The Lord is always ready to draw near. Covenant living opens the door.

Today, take one step closer to God. Let your covenant promises guide your desire to feel His nearness.

What helps you feel close to God as you live your covenants?

July 28

> *"Appoint among yourselves a teacher, and let not all be spokesmen at once; but let one speak at a time and let all listen unto his sayings, that when all have spoken that all may be edified of all, and that every man may have an equal privilege."*
>
> Doctrine and Covenants 88:122

Covenants are not just individual. They are also communal. When we make sacred promises, we join a covenant people. A body of Saints who lift, support, and strengthen one another.

Living your covenants means looking outward. It means asking, "Who can I help? Who needs comfort? Who needs Christ's love today?" Through ministering, temple work, and daily kindness, you fulfill your covenants by blessing others.

One brother said that after being sealed in the temple, he began to see others as part of his eternal family. "It changed the way I served," he said. "I wasn't just helping people. I was honoring my covenant."

Covenant living builds Zion, one act of love at a time.

Today, choose to edify someone. Let your covenants motivate you to strengthen the people around you.

How does living your covenants help you build up the people God has placed in your life?

July 29

> *"Come unto me, all ye that labour and are heavy laden, and I will give you rest."*
> Matthew 11:28

Covenants do not remove the weight of life, but they shift how we carry it. When we yoke ourselves to Christ through sacred promises, we are no longer carrying burdens alone. He walks with us. He strengthens us. He brings rest.

There is peace in knowing you are not expected to do everything on your own. Covenant living is about divine partnership. It is about trusting that when your strength runs out, His grace will continue.

One mother said she often felt overwhelmed by all she needed to do. But as she renewed her covenants each Sunday, she felt calm. "It was my reminder that I wasn't doing this alone," she said. "I was yoked to the Savior."

The promise of rest is real. And it comes through Christ.

Today, bring your burdens to the Savior. Let your covenants remind you that He is walking beside you.

What does it look like for you to find rest in Christ through your covenant relationship with Him?

July 30

> *"Fear none of those things which thou shalt suffer: ... be thou faithful unto death, and I will give thee a crown of life."*
>
> Revelation 2:10

Covenants are not just about this life. They prepare us for eternity. As we remain faithful, the Lord prepares a place for us with Him. Eternal life is not just a destination. It is the fulfillment of every promise God has made to His covenant people.

Faithfulness does not mean perfection. It means perseverance. It means returning again and again to the Savior, trusting in His grace, and striving to keep the promises we have made.

One elderly sister said she had spent decades trying to live her covenants. "It wasn't always easy," she said, "but it was always worth it. Now I feel ready. I know the Lord knows my heart."

To be faithful to your covenants is to walk with God. And that path leads to home.

Today, reflect on the eternal perspective of your covenants. Let that vision inspire steady, faithful living.

What helps you stay faithful as you look toward the eternal promises of God?

July 31

> *"See, I have set before thee this day life and good, and death and evil; ... therefore choose life, that both thou and thy seed may live:"*
> Deuteronomy 30:15, 19

Covenants invite us to choose life. Not just physical life, but spiritual vitality, purpose, and divine direction. Every time we choose to keep a commandment, offer service, or turn to Christ, we are choosing the abundant life He offers.

That life is filled with peace, even in trials. It is filled with joy, even in the ordinary. It is filled with light, because it is rooted in the Savior's love.

One young adult said that when she focused on her covenants, her life felt more clear. "I had more direction. I knew what mattered. It helped me say yes to the things that brought me closer to Christ."

Covenant living is choosing the life God has prepared for you. A life full of grace, purpose, and eternal promise.

Today, choose life. Let your covenants help you focus on what brings peace and lasting joy.

How can you more fully embrace the abundant life offered through your covenant path?

August

Seek to become like Christ by cultivating virtue, embracing humility, and receiving His spiritual gifts.

August 1

> "... Therefore, what manner of men ought ye to be? Verily I say unto you, even as I am."
>
> 3 Nephi 27:27

THE CALL TO DISCIPLESHIP is also a call to transformation. Becoming like Christ is not something we achieve in a day. It is something we pursue day by day, with grace and steady effort. He does not ask us to become Him all at once. He invites us to follow Him, to walk with Him, and to let His Spirit shape who we are becoming.

Virtue, humility, and spiritual strength are not just ideals. They are gifts cultivated through practice and prayer. As we spend more time with the Savior in scripture, prayer, and in the temple, we begin to reflect His character in small, sincere ways.

One young man said he used to feel overwhelmed by the idea of becoming like Christ. "But then I realized it's a journey. I just have to keep choosing Him, and He'll help me become more than I am now."

Christ does not expect perfection. He simply asks for a willing heart.

Today, choose one Christlike trait to focus on. Let the Spirit guide your efforts to grow in it.

What helps you remember that becoming like Christ is a journey, not a destination?

August 2

> *"Let thy bowels also be full of charity towards all men, and to the household of faith, and let virtue garnish thy thoughts unceasingly; then shall thy confidence wax strong in the presence of God; and the doctrine of the priesthood shall distil upon thy soul as the dews from heaven."*
> Doctrine and Covenants 121:45

Becoming like Christ begins with our thoughts. Virtue is not just about avoiding sin. It is about filling our minds and hearts with what is pure, uplifting, and holy. As we invite virtue into our thoughts, we begin to feel greater peace, clarity, and spiritual confidence.

Virtuous living does not mean flawless thinking. It means intentional thinking. It means noticing what we dwell on and choosing what invites the Spirit.

One sister said she started being more aware of the media she consumed and the conversations she joined. "The change wasn't dramatic, but it was deep. I felt lighter, and I felt more connected to the Spirit."

Virtue invites the presence of God. It prepares our hearts to hear Him and reflect Him.

Today, pay attention to your thoughts. Choose something virtuous to focus on and let it lift your spirit.

How does increasing virtue in your life help you feel closer to Christ?

August 3

> *"But it shall not be so among you: but whosoever will be great among you, let him be your minister;"*
>
> Matthew 20:26

Christlike greatness is not measured in status or success. It is measured in humility and service. The Savior's path was one of lifting others, noticing the overlooked, and loving without condition. To become like Him is to serve like Him.

Humility is not thinking less of ourselves. It is thinking more about others. It is letting go of pride, comparison, and the need for recognition. True discipleship is quiet, steady, and often unseen.

One young adult said he started praying each morning, "Help me see someone I can serve today." He said, "It changed how I walked through my day. I wasn't just thinking about myself. I was trying to live like Christ."

Greatness in the Lord's kingdom looks like grace, compassion, and a willingness to serve.

Today, serve someone without expecting anything in return. Let your humility draw you closer to Christ.

What is one way you can practice Christlike humility in your relationships this week?

August 4

> *"For the natural man is an enemy to God, and has been from the fall of Adam, and will be, forever and ever, unless he yields to the enticings of the Holy Spirit, ..."*
>
> Mosiah 3:19

Becoming like Christ requires yielding. It means choosing to let go of pride, anger, selfishness, or fear, and allowing the Spirit to shape something holier in its place. We do not overcome the natural man by willpower alone. We do it by surrendering to God's power.

Yielding is not weakness. It is strength rooted in trust. It is saying, "I want to be more like the Savior," and then being willing to change, even when it is uncomfortable.

One brother said he began catching himself when he wanted to react in frustration. "I'd pause and pray instead. That one change helped me feel more peace."

The Spirit can only shape what we are willing to place in His hands.

Today, ask the Lord what part of your natural self He wants to refine. Yield to His guidance with trust.

What does it mean to you to yield to the Spirit in your daily discipleship?

August 5

> *"... seek ye earnestly the best gifts, always remembering for what they are given;"*
> Doctrine and Covenants 46:8

Spiritual gifts are not just blessings. They are tools for becoming. They help us serve, comfort, teach, and grow. And they are given to all who seek them in faith.

You may not feel like you have remarkable gifts. But the Lord sees your potential, and He gives you what you need to fulfill your purpose. Sometimes gifts appear as talents. Sometimes they come as quiet strengths—discernment, patience, compassion.

One woman shared that she never considered herself spiritually gifted until someone thanked her for always listening without judgment. "I realized that was something God had given me," she said. "And I could use it to bless others."

Every spiritual gift is sacred when used to build His kingdom.

Today, pray to recognize one spiritual gift you have been given. Use it to bless someone else.

How can seeking and using spiritual gifts help you become more like the Savior?

August 6

> "And by the power of the Holy Ghost ye may know the truth of all things."
>
> Moroni 10:5

Becoming like Christ means learning to trust the Holy Ghost as your guide. He is the voice that points you toward truth, reminds you of your identity, and gently corrects you when you stray. His companionship is one of the Savior's greatest gifts.

Sometimes revelation comes in quiet impressions. Sometimes it comes in clarity. But it always leads us closer to Christ. As you learn to listen and act on promptings, you become more sensitive to spiritual things.

One young adult said she started writing down any impressions she felt during scripture study. "Over time, I noticed patterns. The Spirit was teaching me and guiding me all along. I just hadn't been paying close enough attention."

Discipleship grows as your relationship with the Spirit deepens.

Today, ask the Holy Ghost to teach you something specific. Write down what you feel.

How has the Holy Ghost helped you become more like the Savior?

August 7

> *"Let this mind be in you, which was also in Christ Jesus:"*
>
> Philippians 2:5

To become like Christ, we must begin to think like Christ. That does not mean we stop being ourselves. It means our thoughts become more kind, more patient, more forgiving, and more full of grace.

Christlike thinking takes effort. It means catching the pride, the judgment, or the fear early and choosing a higher thought. The more we fill our minds with His words, the more natural it becomes to think as He would.

One man said he began pausing before reacting to difficult situations and asking, "What would Christ think right now?" He said, "It helped me stay calmer, more focused on love than on being right."

Changing how you think is a powerful way to change who you are.

Today, pause and examine your thoughts. Choose to think like Christ would in one situation.

What helps you align your thoughts with the mind of Christ?

August 8

> *"But the fruit of the Spirit is love, joy, peace, longsuffering, gentleness, goodness, faith."*
> Galatians 5:22

The more we walk with the Spirit, the more our lives begin to bear His fruit. These Christlike attributes—love, joy, peace, and more—are not traits we manufacture on our own. They are gifts that grow in a heart aligned with God.

Becoming like Christ is not about forced behavior. It is about becoming the kind of person who naturally reflects His light. As we invite the Spirit into our decisions, conversations, and thoughts, we begin to notice more joy and gentleness in how we live.

One woman said that during a time of great stress, she kept asking for peace. "I didn't get less busy," she said. "But I did feel more calm. The Spirit was with me. That changed how I handled everything."

The fruit of the Spirit is the evidence of a Christ-centered life.

Today, focus on one fruit of the Spirit you want to grow. Ask the Lord to help you cultivate it.

What evidence of the Spirit do you see in your life right now?

August 9

> *"And if men come unto me I will show unto them their weakness. I give unto men weakness that they may be humble; and my grace is sufficient for all men that humble themselves before me;..."*
>
> Ether 12:27

Becoming like Christ includes facing our weaknesses with honesty and hope. Weakness is not something to hide or be ashamed of. It is something to bring to the Savior. He does not show us our flaws to discourage us. He shows them so He can heal and transform us.

Through grace, weaknesses become chances for growth. When we come to Christ, He helps us see how our weaknesses can become strengths. He does this by teaching us through them.

One young man said he struggled with patience until he started asking the Lord to help him grow in it. "It didn't change overnight," he said. "But little by little, the Lord helped me respond with more calm and more love."

Weakness is not the end of your story. It is where Christ begins to work.

Today, ask the Lord how your greatest weakness can become your greatest lesson. Trust Him with the process.

How has the Savior helped you grow through your weaknesses?

August 10

> *"For whom the Lord loveth he chasteneth, ..."*
> Hebrews 12:6

Correction is a sign of divine love. The Lord does not point out our need to change because He is disappointed. He does it because He is deeply invested in who we are becoming. Chastening, when received with humility, becomes a tool for transformation.

Becoming like Christ includes being willing to be corrected. The Spirit often speaks through moments of discomfort, nudging us toward something better. That guidance is not condemnation. It is care.

One sister said she felt a quiet rebuke during a talk at church. "At first, I felt discouraged," she said. "But then I realized it was the Spirit showing me where I could grow. That realization felt more like love than judgment."

Spiritual growth often begins at the moment we choose to listen and change.

Today, notice if the Spirit is correcting you in any way. Receive it with gratitude and a desire to grow.

How do you feel the love of the Lord through correction and redirection?

August 11

> *"Wherefore, be not weary in well-doing, for ye are laying the foundation of a great work. And out of small things proceedeth that which is great."*
>
> Doctrine and Covenants 64:33

Becoming like the Savior happens in small, simple moments. It is not usually the result of grand gestures. It is the accumulation of daily choices to be kind, to forgive, to speak gently, and to serve without expecting anything in return.

We sometimes underestimate the power of small spiritual habits. But the Lord does not. Every quiet act of obedience and faith is counted and magnified by Him.

One young adult said she kept a journal of "small victories," moments when she chose Christ over convenience. "Looking back," she said, "those small things added up. I could see how I was changing."

You are becoming like Him, one quiet decision at a time.

Today, choose one small act of Christlike living and do it with intention. Let it shape who you are becoming.

What small spiritual habit has made a big difference in your discipleship?

August 12

> *"If any of you lack wisdom, let him ask of God, that giveth to all men liberally, and upbraideth not; and it shall be given him."*
>
> James 1:5

Becoming like Christ means learning to turn to the Father for wisdom, just as the Savior did. Humility opens the door to revelation. It is the quiet recognition that we do not have all the answers, but we know where to find them.

Asking God for guidance is not a sign of weakness. It is a sign of strength and faith. He is always willing to teach, lead, and give liberally to those who ask sincerely.

One brother said he started making prayer part of every decision, no matter how small. "The more I asked, the more I recognized His voice," he said. "God didn't just guide me. He changed me."

Seeking wisdom is not just about knowing what to do. It is about becoming someone who walks closely with God.

Today, ask God for wisdom in one area of your life. Listen for His answer, and act in faith.

How does asking for divine guidance help shape your character?

August 13

> *"But he that is greatest among you shall be your servant."*
>
> Matthew 23:11

True greatness in the Lord's kingdom looks nothing like worldly fame. It looks like quiet service, unnoticed kindness, and a willingness to lift others no matter the cost. Christ showed us that the path to greatness is paved with humility.

To become like Him, we must serve like Him with joy, love, and without expectation of reward. Every time you serve, you step into His pattern of living.

One woman said that after a hard day, she brought a meal to a friend who was struggling. "It didn't fix my day," she said, "but it changed my heart. I felt closer to Christ."

Service does not just bless others. It refines us.

Today, choose to serve someone in a quiet way. Let your humility draw you nearer to the Savior.

How has serving others helped you become more like Christ?

August 14

> *"He that is faithful in that which is least is faithful also in much: and he that is unjust in the least is unjust also in much."*
>
> Luke 16:10

Spiritual growth happens in the unnoticed places. Becoming like Christ often begins in the small, daily decisions. The ones no one sees. When we choose honesty, patience, or kindness in simple situations, we build the foundation for deeper discipleship.

Faithfulness in the little things trains our hearts to respond more like His. It creates a life of quiet strength, ready for greater responsibility when the Lord calls.

One young man said he began treating his work and relationships as opportunities to practice discipleship. "I stopped separating spiritual things from everyday things," he said. "That changed how I lived."

Great spiritual growth often begins in ordinary faithfulness.

Today, be intentional in something small. Let your quiet choices reflect your desire to be like Christ.

What does faithfulness in small things look like in your life right now?

August 15

"Christlike attributes are gifts from God. [These attributes] come as [we] use [our] agency righteously. ...With a desire to please God, [we have to] recognize [our] weaknesses and be willing and anxious to improve."
Elder Ulisses Soares

You do not need a spotlight to shine. The quiet power of a Christlike life is one of the strongest ways to influence the world. Humility, gentleness, and love do more to change hearts than arguments or pressure ever could.

When others see patience in stress, compassion in conflict, and light in your countenance, they see Christ through you. That is the kind of influence that lasts.

One sister said she felt drawn to the gospel because of a coworker who never preached, but always radiated peace. "I wanted what she had," she said. "Later I found out it was her faith."

You reflect Christ best by living like Him.

Today, let your example be your testimony. Live with the kind of grace that invites others to know the Savior.

How can your daily example reflect the quiet power of true discipleship?

August 16

> *"Create in me a clean heart, O God; and renew a right spirit within me."*
>
> Psalm 51:10

Becoming like the Savior begins in the heart. A clean heart is not a flawless one, it is a humble one. It is a heart that is willing to be changed, willing to be led, and willing to be softened by grace.

We are not expected to perfect ourselves. But we are invited to let God work within us. That kind of inner renewal happens through prayer, repentance, and sincere desire. As our hearts change, our lives begin to reflect the light of Christ.

One young woman said she started asking in prayer, "What in my heart needs cleansing?" She said, "The answers came gently. And so did the strength to change."

The Savior does not just cleanse sins. He renews spirits.

Today, ask the Lord to create a clean heart within you. Let Him show you what can be renewed.

What part of your heart is ready for healing or change through Christ?

August 17

> *"Because the Melchizedek Priesthood has been restored, both covenant-keeping women and men have access to all the spiritual blessings of the church or, we might say, to all the spiritual treasures the Lord has for His children."*
>
> President Russell M. Nelson

Spiritual gifts are real. They are not rare blessings for the few, they are divine tools given to those who seek them with faith. When you live your covenants, you are eligible to receive power and gifts from God that help you fulfill your unique mission.

These gifts vary. Some are quiet, like wisdom or mercy. Others are more visible, like teaching or healing. All are sacred. And all are given to draw us closer to Christ.

One brother said that as he studied spiritual gifts, he started recognizing them in others, and in himself. "It made me realize we're all needed. We all have something divine to offer."

You are already gifted. The Lord is ready to help you develop and use those gifts.

Today, ask the Lord to help you recognize one spiritual gift you have been given. Seek ways to use it in His service.

How can you better honor and develop the gifts the Lord has given you?

August 18

> *"And charity suffereth long, and is kind, and envieth not, and is not puffed up, seeketh not her own, is not easily provoked, thinketh no evil, and rejoiceth not in iniquity but rejoiceth in the truth, beareth all things, believeth all things, hopeth all things, endureth all things."*
> Moroni 7:45

Charity is more than kindness. It is the pure love of Christ, and it is the foundation of becoming like Him. It shows up in how we treat people who are hard to love, in how we respond when we are hurt, and in how we see others as God sees them.

We do not develop charity overnight. It grows as we practice patience, forgiveness, and grace in daily life. It expands as we let go of pride and allow the Spirit to fill our hearts with Christ's love.

One man said that as he began praying to have more charity, his view of people started to change. "I wasn't as quick to judge," he said. "I started seeing the good first."

Charity is not just a trait, it is a transformation.

Today, ask the Lord to help you love someone a little more like He does.

What does charity look like in your life right now, and how can you let it grow?

August 19

> *"Humble yourselves in the sight of the Lord, and he shall lift you up."*
>
> James 4:10

Humility invites divine strength. It is not weakness. It is the quiet confidence that comes from relying on the Lord instead of your own power. When you humble yourself, you create space for God to teach you, guide you, and lift you higher than you could go alone.

Becoming like Christ begins with becoming teachable. He was perfect, yet He still submitted to the will of the Father. We follow His example not by knowing everything, but by being willing to be shaped by heaven.

One sister shared that she started asking the Lord, "What do I still need to learn?" instead of just asking for help. "It changed how I prayed," she said. "It helped me grow."

The Lord lifts those who bow their hearts before Him.

Today, practice humility in one small way. Let it open your heart to the Lord's refining hand.

How does humility help you become more like the Savior?

August 20

> *"Yea, and cry unto God for all thy support; yea, let all thy doings be unto the Lord, and whithersoever thou goest let it be in the Lord; yea, let all thy thoughts be directed unto the Lord; yea, let the affections of thy heart be placed upon the Lord forever."*
>
> Alma 37:36

Becoming like Christ begins in the mind. When your thoughts are centered on Him, your choices start to reflect His light. This doesn't mean every thought must be deeply spiritual, but it does mean that the Lord becomes the focus behind your intentions, goals, and desires.

Directing your thoughts to the Savior invites clarity and peace. It allows the Spirit to influence your decisions, and it creates space for revelation to guide your steps.

One young woman said she began the habit of repeating Christ-centered affirmations each morning. "It helped me start the day with focus," she said. "It changed how I saw myself and how I treated others."

A Christ-centered mind leads to a Christ-shaped life.

Today, choose to direct your thoughts to the Lord in one part of your day. Watch how it shifts your perspective.

How can you invite more Christ-centered thinking into your everyday routine?

August 21

> *"Pride is a switch that turns off priesthood power. Humility is a switch that turns it on. ... We don't discover humility by thinking less of ourselves; we discover humility by thinking less about ourselves."*
>
> Elder Dieter F. Uchtdorf

Humility is a defining trait of the Savior. It is not about feeling small or unworthy. It is about lifting others, submitting to God's will, and seeing yourself clearly as a child of God with divine potential.

As you become more humble, you begin to let go of pride and pressure. You listen more. You compare less. You focus more on helping and less on impressing. That is where Christlike character grows.

One brother said he began recognizing pride in subtle ways, like needing recognition or pushing his own plans. "When I asked for humility," he said, "the Lord helped me see others more clearly. It softened me."

Humility makes room for revelation and deeper connection with God and others.

Today, choose one way to focus less on yourself and more on the Savior. Let humility shape your thoughts.

How can humility help you become more like Christ in your words and actions?

August 22

> *"And when he had said these words, he wept, and the multitude bare record of it, and he took their little children, one by one, and blessed them, and prayed unto the Father for them."*
>
> 3 Nephi 17:21

Christ's love is deeply personal. He does not love us in groups or categories. He sees each of us individually, and He ministers one by one. To become like Him is to slow down, to see people as He does, and to offer presence instead of performance.

Sometimes the most powerful way to reflect the Savior is to truly notice someone, to listen, to offer a kind word, or to lift a burden quietly.

One sister said that during a difficult season, someone simply sat with her and said, "You're not alone." She said, "That moment felt like Christ Himself was with me."

Christlike love does not require grand gestures. It simply requires attention.

Today, be present for someone in a meaningful way. Look for the one the Lord would have you reach.

What changes in your relationships when you love people one by one?

August 23

> *"And he gave some, apostles; and some, prophets; and some, evangelists; and some, pastors and teachers; For the perfecting of the saints, for the work of the ministry, for the edifying of the body of Christ:"*
>
> Ephesians 4:11–12

Spiritual gifts are given to build the body of Christ. We are not meant to be the same. We are meant to be unified through diversity. Each person brings something unique, and every gift matters in the work of the Lord.

You may not always recognize your gifts right away, but God does. As you live faithfully, He reveals them. And as you use them, He multiplies them.

One young man said he often compared himself to others at church. "Then someone thanked me for how I made them feel welcome," he said. "I realized that was my gift, and it mattered."

There is no small role in God's kingdom.

Today, express gratitude for one spiritual gift you've seen in someone else. Let it inspire you to use your own.

How can you use your unique gifts to strengthen the body of Christ?

August 24

> *"And behold, I tell you these things that ye may learn wisdom; that ye may learn that when ye are in the service of your fellow beings ye are only in the service of your God."*
> Mosiah 2:17

One of the clearest ways to become like Christ is to serve as He did. His life was filled with quiet acts of compassion, healing, teaching, lifting, and loving. When we choose to serve, especially in small and consistent ways, we reflect His light more clearly.

Service is not about convenience or recognition. It is about love in action. And often, it is through service that we discover spiritual gifts we did not know we had.

One woman shared that she never felt comfortable teaching or speaking, but she found joy in sending thoughtful notes and checking in on people. "It's how I show love," she said. "And I feel close to the Savior when I do."

Christlike service blesses others, and it transforms us.

Today, look for a small way to serve someone with love. Let your service draw you closer to Christ.

How has serving others helped you recognize the Savior's presence in your life?

August 25

> *"Blessed are the pure in heart: for they shall see God."*
>
> Matthew 5:8

Purity of heart is not about perfection. It is about sincerity. It is about living with honest intent, clean desires, and a willing spirit. When our hearts are centered on God, our vision clears. We begin to see His hand more clearly, and we feel His presence more often.

The world may cloud our hearts with distractions and noise, but a pure heart seeks stillness, connection, and truth. And it invites the Spirit to stay.

One young adult said she began each day with a simple prayer: "Help me keep my heart clean today." She said, "It didn't make me flawless, but it helped me be more aware and more at peace."

A pure heart opens the door to deeper revelation and greater closeness with God.

Today, choose one way to cleanse or guard your heart. Let that choice bring you closer to the Savior.

What does a pure heart look like in your daily decisions and desires?

August 26

> *"The Spirit itself beareth witness with our spirit, that we are the children of God:"*
> Romans 8:16

To become like Christ, we must first understand who we truly are. We are not just disciples. We are beloved children of God. That identity is the foundation of all spiritual growth. When we remember our divine heritage, we live with more purpose, more peace, and more confidence in who we are becoming.

The Spirit confirms this truth in quiet, sacred moments. And the more we turn to God, the more deeply that truth settles into our hearts.

One brother shared that when he felt unworthy and overwhelmed, he repeated the phrase, "I am a child of God." "It didn't fix everything," he said, "but it helped me stand up and try again."

Becoming like Christ begins with believing you are already loved by Him.

Today, remind yourself of your divine identity. Let that truth guide your thoughts and actions.

How does remembering you are a child of God help you walk the path of discipleship?

August 27

> *"Behold, the Lord requireth the heart and a willing mind; ..."*
> Doctrine and Covenants 64:34

The Lord does not expect perfection. He invites participation. A willing mind and a faithful heart are enough to begin. As we offer what we have—our time, our effort, our desires—He magnifies it into something more.

Spiritual progress often begins with willingness. Willingness to change. Willingness to forgive. Willingness to follow. As you become more willing, you become more like the Savior, who gave His whole heart to the Father's will.

One sister said she felt inadequate in a new Church calling. "But I prayed and told the Lord I was willing," she said. "That willingness opened the door for Him to teach and help me."

Willingness is where miracles begin.

Today, offer the Lord a willing heart. Trust that He will guide your next step.

What is one way you can show the Lord your willingness to grow today?

August 28

> *"And as I have prayed among you even so shall ye pray in my church, among my people who do repent and are baptized in my name. Behold I am the light; I have set an example for you."*
> 3 Nephi 18:16

The Savior never asked us to do anything He was not willing to do Himself. His life is the perfect pattern. He showed us how to pray, how to forgive, how to love, and how to endure. Becoming like Him begins with following His example, one step at a time.

We will not always get it right. But each time we choose to act as He would, we draw closer to His light and invite more of His presence into our lives.

One young woman said she started reading the Gospels with one question in mind: "What can I learn from how Jesus responds?" She said, "It made the scriptures come alive and gave me something to practice every day."

Christ is not only our Redeemer. He is our model for daily living.

Today, choose one Christlike behavior to practice more intentionally. Let His example guide you.

How does following the Savior's example help you grow into His likeness?

August 29

"Let no man despise thy youth; but be thou an example of the believers, in word, in conversation, in charity, in spirit, in faith, in purity."

1 Timothy 4:12

Becoming like Christ is not only about what we believe. It is about how we live. Our words, our actions, and our attitude all testify of who we follow. When we live with integrity and love, we become examples of the believers in a world that deeply needs light.

You may never know who is watching or who is being influenced by your quiet discipleship. But God knows. And He uses your example in ways you may not see.

One brother shared that his neighbor started asking gospel questions after watching how he treated his family. "He said it was the peace he saw in our home that made him curious," he said.

Your example can open hearts and point others to Christ.

Today, let your everyday actions reflect what you believe. Be a living testimony of discipleship.

In what ways can your daily life become a clearer example of the Savior's teachings?

August 30

> *"How God anointed Jesus of Nazareth with the Holy Ghost and with power: who went about doing good, and healing all that were oppressed of the devil; for God was with him."*
> Acts 10:38

This simple phrase captures the life of Jesus Christ. He did not seek recognition. He did not wait for perfect timing. He simply moved through life with compassion, awareness, and love. To become like Him is to do the same.

Goodness is quiet, steady, and powerful. It shows up in small choices, a kind word, a patient response, a helping hand. When we consistently do good, we reflect His nature and draw others to Him.

One woman said she began ending each day by asking, "Did I do good today?" She said, "It wasn't about being perfect. It was about being intentional. And it helped me live more like Christ."

Becoming like the Savior does not always mean doing great things. It means doing good things with great love.

Today, go about doing good. Let your actions reflect the goodness of the One you follow.

What small good can you do today to reflect the heart of Christ?

August 31

> *"And I will also be your light in the wilderness; and I will prepare the way before you, if it so be that ye shall keep my commandments; wherefore, inasmuch as ye shall keep my commandments ye shall be led towards the promised land; and ye shall know that it is by me that ye are led."*
>
> 1 Nephi 17:13

The path to becoming like Christ is not always easy. It will include wilderness moments, times of uncertainty, struggle, or waiting. But the Lord promises to be our light in those places. He walks with us, teaches us, and shapes us in ways we cannot always see.

The wilderness is not the end of the journey. It is part of the transformation. It is where we come to know the Savior more deeply and where we become more like Him.

One young man shared that during a hard trial, he felt the Savior's presence more than ever before. "It didn't remove the pain," he said, "but it reminded me I wasn't alone. That gave me strength."

Christ's light does not always take us out of the wilderness. Sometimes, it helps us walk through it.

Today, look for the Savior's light in your personal wilderness. Trust that He is guiding you forward.

How has the Lord's light helped you become more like Him during difficult seasons?

September

Walk with Christ each day and draw strength to endure through His sustaining grace.

September 1

> *"And now, my beloved brethren, I would that ye should come unto Christ, who is the Holy One of Israel, and partake of his salvation, and the power of his redemption. Yea, come unto him, and offer your whole souls as an offering unto him, and continue in fasting and praying, and endure to the end; and as the Lord liveth ye will be saved."*
>
> Omni 1:26

WALKING WITH CHRIST BEGINS with coming to Him every day, in every season, just as you are. This is not a one-time decision. It is a daily return. A choice to let Him guide your steps and strengthen your soul.

Endurance in the gospel is not about never feeling weak. It is about returning to the Savior again and again, trusting that His power is enough to lift, renew, and redeem.

One sister said she kept this verse on her mirror. "I read it each morning to remind myself that today, I can come to Him again," she said. "That's how I keep walking."

Walking with Christ means choosing Him even when the path feels steep.

Today, come to Christ in a simple and sincere way. Let His presence steady your steps.

What helps you begin your day with the Savior and draw on His power throughout it?

September 2

> *"But they that wait upon the Lord shall renew their strength; they shall mount up with wings as eagles; they shall run, and not be weary; and they shall walk, and not faint."*
>
> Isaiah 40:31

Endurance is often quiet. It looks like waiting in faith when answers don't come quickly. It looks like continuing forward when the outcome is uncertain. But with the Lord, waiting is never wasted. It becomes a time of renewal.

Those who walk with Christ do not rely on their own strength alone. They wait on Him. They trust in His timing. And as they do, they find strength they didn't know they had.

One brother said that during a prolonged trial, he stopped asking "Why?" and started praying, "Help me wait with faith." He said, "That shift brought peace. And the strength came, slowly, but surely."

Endurance is not just holding on. It is holding on with hope.

Today, trust that the Lord is renewing your strength, even in the waiting. Let that hope carry you forward.

How has the Lord strengthened you during times of spiritual or emotional waiting?

September 3

> *"And whoso receiveth you, there I will be also, for I will go before your face. I will be on your right hand and on your left, and my Spirit shall be in your hearts, and mine angels round about you, to bear you up."*
> Doctrine and Covenants 84:88

You never walk alone. When you choose to walk with the Savior, He surrounds you with His presence. He goes before you to prepare the way. He stands beside you to strengthen and steady you. And He walks behind you to lift you when you fall.

Knowing this changes how we face our challenges. It doesn't remove them, but it brings courage and calm. It reminds us that the strength we need is already walking with us.

One woman said that when she felt overwhelmed by everything ahead of her, she whispered this scripture to herself. "It helped me keep going," she said. "Because I knew He was already there."

Christ does not just send help. He is the help.

Today, walk with the assurance that Christ goes before you. Let His presence replace your fear.

What difference does it make to know the Savior walks every step with you?

September 4

> *"And it came to pass that I, Nephi, said unto my father: I will go and do the things which the Lord hath commanded, for I know that the Lord giveth no commandments unto the children of men, save he shall prepare a way for them that they may accomplish the thing which he commandeth them."*
>
> 1 Nephi 3:7

Endurance often begins with a willing heart. Nephi didn't know exactly how the Lord would provide a way, he just trusted that He would. That trust became the strength that carried him forward through every unknown.

Sometimes the next step feels unclear or too hard. But when we are willing to go and do, even without all the answers, the Lord responds with grace, guidance, and help.

One young woman said she chose this verse as her theme during a challenging semester. "Every day I said it out loud," she said. "It gave me the courage to move forward, one faithful step at a time."

Endurance is built on small, consistent acts of trust.

Today, offer the Lord a willing heart. Take the next faithful step, even if you don't see the full path.

How has trusting the Lord helped you keep going through the unknown?

September 5

> *"Look unto me in every thought; doubt not, fear not."*
>
> Doctrine and Covenants 6:36

When life feels uncertain, the invitation is simple and powerful: *look to Christ*. Not just occasionally, but in every thought. As we turn our focus to Him through prayer, scripture, worship, and quiet reflection, our doubts begin to fade and our fears lose their grip.

Looking to Christ doesn't mean pretending everything is fine. It means trusting that He is. It means fixing our eyes on the One who calms storms, heals hearts, and never turns away.

One brother said he started pausing during the day to whisper a simple prayer: "I'm looking to You." He said, "It helped re-center my mind and remind me I'm not alone."

The more we look to Him, the more clearly we see the way forward.

Today, look to Christ when fear or doubt begins to rise. Let Him steady your thoughts and your heart.

What helps you keep your focus on the Savior when life feels overwhelming?

September 6

> "... let us run with patience the race that is set before us, Looking unto Jesus the author and finisher of our faith; ..."
>
> Hebrews 12:1-2

The path of discipleship is not a sprint. It is a lifelong race. It requires patience, endurance, and trust that the Lord is both the beginning and the end of the journey. He knows your path. He runs it with you. And He will finish what He started in you.

There will be moments when you feel tired or tempted to give up. In those moments, look again to the Savior. He understands what it means to keep going, even when the way is hard.

One woman said she wrote this verse on a sticky note and put it on her treadmill. "It reminded me that spiritual endurance matters more than speed," she said. "And that Jesus is running beside me."

You are not alone in your race. Christ is your strength and your companion.

Today, choose to run with patience. Trust that each step forward matters in your journey of faith.

What helps you stay spiritually steady when the path is long?

September 7

> *"And lo, I am with thee, even unto the end of thy days; for thou shalt deliver my people from bondage, even Israel my chosen."*
>
> Moses 1:26

God's promises are often quiet, but they are never uncertain. One of His clearest and most repeated assurances is this: *He will be with you*. In your progress and in your pain. In your clarity and in your confusion. He does not leave.

When the road feels long, that promise becomes an anchor. Walking with Christ does not mean life will be easy. It means you will never face it alone.

One young man said he repeated this phrase to himself during a difficult transition: "Nevertheless, I will be with you." He said, "It was the reminder I needed to just keep moving forward."

His presence is constant. His companionship is real. His love is what keeps us going.

Today, pause and remember His promise to stay with you. Let that truth renew your hope.

How does knowing God is with you change how you face today's challenges?

September 8

> *"Now ye may suppose that this is foolishness in me; but behold I say unto you, that by small and simple things are great things brought to pass; and small means in many instances doth confound the wise."*
>
> Alma 37:6

Endurance is built in small, simple ways. It grows through daily prayers, honest efforts, and quiet faith. The most powerful spiritual strength is not flashy or fast. It is steady. It shows up day after day, no matter how ordinary the moment feels.

Walking with the Savior is not always dramatic. Most days, it looks like choosing good over easy, turning to Him in stillness, and doing what's right without needing applause.

One sister said she used to think her efforts didn't count unless they were big. "But I've learned that small things matter deeply to God," she said. "He sees them. And He multiplies them."

Small spiritual habits create strong disciples.

Today, do one small act of discipleship with faith. Trust that it matters more than you know.

What simple daily practice helps you stay strong in your walk with Christ?

September 9

> *"Have not I commanded thee? Be strong and of a good courage; be not afraid, neither be thou dismayed: for the Lord thy God is with thee whithersoever thou goest."*
>
> Joshua 1:9

Courage is not the absence of fear. It is the quiet determination to move forward with faith, even when the future feels uncertain. When you walk with the Lord, your strength is not your own. His presence becomes your courage.

You do not need to have everything figured out to keep going. You simply need to trust the One who walks beside you.

One sister said this verse helped her during a season of decision-making. "I didn't know what was coming," she said, "but I knew God was with me. That made me brave."

Endurance comes when we remember who is walking with us.

Today, choose to move forward in faith, even if you feel unsure. Let the Lord's presence give you courage.

When have you felt God's strength helping you face something uncertain?

September 10

> *"Wherefore, be not weary in well-doing, for ye are laying the foundation of a great work. And out of small things proceedeth that which is great."*
>
> Doctrine and Covenants 64:33

It is easy to feel tired when your efforts seem unnoticed or slow to bear fruit. But the Lord sees what you are building. He sees the prayers, the kindness, the steady service. And He calls it great work.

Endurance in discipleship means choosing to keep doing good, even when results are delayed. It means trusting that every act of faith is part of something eternal.

One mother said this verse helped her on hard days. "It reminded me that raising a child in the gospel is a great work, even when it's messy," she said.

Your faithfulness matters more than you know.

Today, press forward in your quiet good work. Trust that the Lord is building something beautiful through you.

What helps you keep going when your efforts feel small or slow?

September 11

> *"Peace I leave with you, my peace I give unto you: not as the world giveth, give I unto you. Let not your heart be troubled, neither let it be afraid."*
>
> John 14:27

The peace of Christ is different from anything the world offers. It is not based on perfect circumstances. It comes in the middle of them. His peace calms fears, quiets the heart, and steadies us in the middle of hard things.

Enduring with Christ means learning to rely on His peace when life feels heavy. It means letting His words soothe your worries and trusting that He has not left you alone.

One woman said she repeated this verse during nights of worry and overwhelm. "It didn't take the trial away," she said, "but I felt calmer. I felt held."

Peace is not the absence of trouble. It is the presence of the Savior.

Today, ask the Lord for His peace. Let it fill the places where you feel unsettled.

How have you experienced Christ's peace even when life wasn't peaceful?

September 12

> *"Cast thy burden upon the Lord, and he shall sustain thee: ..."*
>
> Psalm 55:22

You were never meant to carry everything alone. The Savior invites you to bring your burdens to Him. Not just in moments of crisis, but in everyday struggles. He does not always remove the weight, but He strengthens you to bear it.

Walking with Him means learning how to lay things down. It means trusting that He can carry what feels too heavy, and that He wants to.

One brother said he started writing down his worries in a notebook and then praying over the list. "It was my way of handing them over," he said. "And I always felt lighter afterward."

The Lord does not just see your burdens. He sustains you through them.

Today, give one worry to the Lord in sincere prayer. Trust Him to hold it for you.

What helps you remember that you don't have to carry everything on your own?

September 13

> *"The Lord is my strength and song, and he is become my salvation: he is my God, and I will prepare him an habitation; my father's God, and I will exalt him."*
>
> Exodus 15:2

There are days when your own strength runs low. That is when the Lord becomes not just your support, but your source of strength. He doesn't just help you endure. He helps you sing through the storm. His presence brings both power and praise.

Endurance with Christ is not silent survival. It is a life filled with quiet hope, even in hardship. He gives more than stamina. He gives a reason to keep rejoicing.

One sister said she started keeping a "strength journal," a place to record moments when she felt the Lord carry her. "I could look back and see His hand every time I thought I couldn't go on," she said.

The Lord is not just your rescue. He is your rejoicing.

Today, thank the Lord for one way He has strengthened you recently. Let that remembrance lift your heart.

What does it look like to praise God even when life is hard?

September 14

> *"In your patience possess ye your souls."*
> Luke 21:19

Patience is more than waiting. It is a spiritual practice. It is the way we keep our souls centered while we move through delay, difficulty, or doubt. In patience, we learn to endure not with resentment, but with peace.

Walking with Christ means letting Him shape your pace, not just your path. Some blessings come quickly. Others take time. Patience allows you to walk faithfully, even when you don't see immediate results.

One sister said she began praying not for answers, but for patience. "That prayer changed me," she said. "It made room for peace, even before the solution came."

Patience is not passive. It is powerful.

Today, practice patience in one aspect of your life that feels slow or uncertain. Invite the Lord to walk with you through it.

Where is the Lord teaching you patience right now?

September 15

> *"And we know that all things work together for good to them that love God, ..."*
> Romans 8:28

Endurance often means holding on when things don't make sense yet. But with Christ, nothing is wasted. Even the hardest seasons can become sacred ground. He weaves trials into strength, questions into understanding, and delays into preparation.

To walk with Him is to trust that even when the road is rough, He is still working for your good.

One man shared that when a long-awaited blessing didn't come, he felt discouraged. But years later, he could see how the delay led to unexpected growth. "God didn't forget me," he said. "He was just building something better."

Faith sees beyond the moment. It trusts that the Lord sees the full picture.

Today, trust that something good is being prepared for you, even if you don't see it yet.

> How has the Lord brought good out of something that once felt hard to endure?

September 16

> *"Behold, the Lord requireth the heart and a willing mind; ..."*
>
> Doctrine and Covenants 64:34

Endurance is not about having endless energy. It is about offering a willing heart. The Lord does not expect you to never feel tired or overwhelmed. He asks only that you keep offering yourself, your intent, your love, and your desire to follow.

When you walk with Him, your offering is always enough. A willing heart opens the door for Him to strengthen, renew, and carry you.

One sister said she whispered this verse to herself when she felt inadequate. "It reminded me that willingness mattered more than perfection," she said. "And that gave me peace."

Your willingness is sacred. It is where miracles begin.

Today, offer the Lord your willing heart, just as it is. Let Him fill in the rest.

What does it mean to you to give the Lord your heart, especially when you feel tired?

September 17

"I can do all things through Christ which strengtheneth me."

Philippians 4:13

This verse is more than a statement of confidence. It is a declaration of reliance. The strength to keep going, to overcome, to endure, all flows from Christ. When we remember that, the pressure to do it all alone begins to lift.

You were never meant to carry everything on your own. Christ doesn't just strengthen the strong. He lifts the weary, the unsure, and the trying.

One woman said she repeated this verse each morning before work. "Some days I didn't believe it right away," she said. "But by the end of the day, I'd always seen how He showed up."

With Christ, strength is never out of reach.

Today, speak this verse aloud in faith. Let it remind you that His strength is always available to you.

When has Christ given you strength beyond your own ability?

September 18

> "... wherefore, continue in patience until ye are perfected."
>
> Doctrine and Covenants 67:13

Becoming like the Savior takes time. It's not a race toward flawlessness, but a steady walk of trust. Patience allows us to endure our imperfections, to forgive ourselves, and to keep going while we grow.

When you walk with Christ, He helps you see progress even when it feels slow. He celebrates your effort and walks beside you with love and grace.

One brother said he used to feel frustrated by how long change took. "But then I realized the Lord wasn't rushing me," he said. "He was walking with me. And that made all the difference."

Spiritual growth is not a finish line. It is a faithful journey.

Today, be patient with your progress. Let the Lord shape you with time, love, and grace.

What helps you stay patient with yourself as you grow closer to Christ?

September 19

> *"... They that be whole need not a physician, but they that are sick."*
>
> Matthew 9:12

The Savior never asked us to be perfect before we came to Him. He invites the weary, the broken, and the burdened to walk with Him. He is not just a companion on the road. He is the Healer who strengthens us as we go.

Endurance includes learning to lean on Him when we feel spiritually or emotionally unwell. His strength is made perfect in our weakness, and His mercy meets us exactly where we are.

One woman said she hesitated to pray during a time of personal struggle. "But when I finally did," she said, "I didn't feel judged. I felt wrapped in love."

You do not have to be whole to walk with Christ. You just have to be willing.

Today, come to the Savior honestly. Let Him walk with you, even if you feel unworthy.

What helps you trust that Christ welcomes you as you are, not just as you hope to be?

September 20

> *"And see that all these things are done in wisdom and order; for it is not requisite that a man should run faster than he has strength. And again, it is expedient that he should be diligent, that thereby he might win the prize; therefore, all things must be done in order."*
>
> Mosiah 4:27

Spiritual endurance isn't about constant speed. It's about sustainable faith. The Lord knows your capacity. He understands your limitations. And He never asks you to do more than He will help you accomplish.

Sometimes we put pressure on ourselves to do everything all at once. But discipleship is a lifelong journey. Christ is more interested in your consistency than your pace.

One young man said he began setting small spiritual goals instead of trying to change everything at once. "It helped me keep going," he said. "I wasn't exhausted, I was growing."

Walking with the Savior means walking wisely. He will help you move forward at the right pace for you.

Today, let go of the pressure to do it all. Focus on doing what you can, with faith and steadiness.

How can you better align your spiritual efforts with what the Lord is actually asking of you?

September 21

> *"The Lord is my shepherd; I shall not want."*
> Psalm 23:1

To walk with the Savior is to walk with a Shepherd. He knows every turn in your path, every burden you carry, and every need of your heart. With Him, you are never lost, never forgotten, never without care.

Endurance becomes possible when you trust that He is guiding you, not to something random, but to something good. He leads you beside still waters. He restores your soul.

One sister said this verse became her anchor during a time of uncertainty. "I didn't know the next step," she said, "but I knew the Shepherd. That gave me peace."

With Christ as your Shepherd, you can keep walking, even through the unknown.

Today, trust that the Savior is leading you. Follow His voice, and let Him comfort your soul.

> **What helps you recognize the Shepherd's guidance in your daily walk?**

September 22

> *"And let us not be weary in well doing: for in due season we shall reap, if we faint not."*
> Galatians 6:9

There will be days when your efforts feel unseen and your strength feels spent. But God sees you. He sees your quiet faith, your daily efforts, your hidden sacrifices. And He promises that the harvest will come, in His time, and in His way.

Endurance in well doing means trusting the process even when the results are slow. It means continuing with faith, knowing that the Lord multiplies what we offer.

One father said he didn't always see the impact of family scripture study. "But years later, I saw my kids repeating those verses. That's when I realized this mattered."

Your daily discipleship is never wasted.

Today, keep doing good, even if no one sees it but the Lord. Trust in the harvest He has promised.

What motivates you to keep going when the results are not yet visible?

September 23

> *"Be patient in afflictions, for thou shalt have many; but endure them, for, lo, I am with thee, even unto the end of thy days."*
> Doctrine and Covenants 24:8

Enduring to the end doesn't mean walking a perfect path. It means choosing to stay close to Christ, especially when things are hard. His promise is not just for today or tomorrow. It's for every step of your life, until the very end.

When you feel tired or discouraged, it's okay to rest in Him. He's not asking for flawless effort. He's asking for your continued heart. And He will walk every step with you.

One woman shared that after a long season of illness, she felt distant from the Lord. "But when I finally opened my scriptures again, I felt Him immediately," she said. "He had never left."

His presence doesn't expire. His companionship is constant.

Today, trust that the Lord is still with you, even if your pace has slowed. He's not going anywhere.

How does the Savior's promise to stay with you bring comfort in your journey?

September 24

> *"When we choose to follow Christ, we choose to be changed."*
>
> President Ezra Taft Benson

Endurance is not just about staying the same. It's about growing. Walking with Christ changes you, not all at once, but over time, through small spiritual choices that shape your heart.

When you walk with Him daily, you become more patient, more hopeful, more like Him. Your trials may not disappear, but your strength will increase.

One woman said that over time, she noticed her reactions shifting. "I was less quick to anger, more quick to pray. I realized I was changing. And it was because of Him."

You are not meant to walk this path unchanged. You are meant to be transformed by it.

Today, notice one way Christ is changing you. Give thanks for your growth, even if it's slow.

What changes have you seen in yourself as you've chosen to walk with Christ?

September 25

> *"For ye have need of patience, that, after ye have done the will of God, ye might receive the promise."*
>
> Hebrews 10:36

Doing the will of God doesn't always bring immediate results. Sometimes the blessings come slowly, through layers of trust and time. Patience is not just a virtue, it is a requirement for receiving the fullness of His promises.

Endurance means continuing to do good even when you cannot yet see the outcome. It means holding to what you know, even when the waiting feels long.

One brother said that after years of praying for a specific blessing, he finally received it, but not in the way he expected. "Looking back," he said, "the waiting taught me things the blessing never could have."

The promises are sure. The timing is divine.

Today, choose to trust the Lord's timeline. Keep doing what is right, and let patience do its perfect work.

What helps you stay faithful while waiting on the Lord's promises?

September 26

> *"Come unto me, all ye that labour and are heavy laden, and I will give you rest."*
> Matthew 11:28

The Lord's invitation to come unto Him is not just for the strong or the sure. It is for the tired, the stretched thin, the quietly struggling. He does not turn away those who are burdened. He welcomes them.

Walking with Christ brings rest, not always in circumstance, but in spirit. He helps you breathe in peace even when life feels full. He steadies your hands, calms your thoughts, and fills your heart with quiet assurance.

One sister said she started reading this verse at the end of each long day. "It helped me remember I didn't have to carry everything alone," she said. "The Lord was carrying me."

You are never too weary to come to Christ.

Today, take a quiet moment to come to the Savior. Let Him give you rest where you need it most.

What would it look like to truly let Christ carry part of your burden today?

September 27

> *"Watch ye, stand fast in the faith, quit you like men, be strong."*
>
> 1 Corinthians 16:13

Enduring with Christ means standing firm, even when the winds of doubt or distraction blow strong. Faith is not passive, it is active. It watches, stands, and holds fast. And through it, you are strengthened beyond your own capacity.

Walking with the Savior builds spiritual resilience. Each test faced with faith deepens your roots and prepares you to lift others who may one day need your strength.

One young man shared that he started reading a verse of scripture each time he felt spiritually tired. "It reminded me I wasn't standing alone," he said. "God was helping me stay grounded."

Faith is not always loud, but it is always powerful.

Today, stand fast in something that matters to your faith. Let the Lord strengthen your resolve.

Where do you feel the Lord helping you stay steady in your discipleship?

September 28

> *"The Lord is good, a strong hold in the day of trouble; and he knoweth them that trust in him."*
>
> Nahum 1:7

When the day feels heavy and answers seem far away, the Lord is your safe place. He doesn't just know your name. He knows your heart, your struggles, and your desire to keep going. And He holds you close.

Walking with Him doesn't guarantee a trouble-free path. But it does guarantee you'll never walk it alone. His goodness is constant, and His strength is always enough.

One sister shared that during a season of deep anxiety, she clung to this verse. "I said it every morning," she said. "It helped me breathe. It reminded me I was known."

Being known by God is one of the deepest forms of comfort.

Today, trust that the Lord sees you, knows you, and will hold you through whatever comes.

How does remembering that the Lord knows you personally strengthen your endurance?

September 29

> *"And the Lord, he it is that doth go before thee; he will be with thee, he will not fail thee, neither forsake thee: fear not, neither be dismayed."*
>
> Deuteronomy 31:8

There will always be moments when the next step feels uncertain. But the Lord never asks you to walk alone. He goes before you. He prepares the path. He surrounds you with His presence, even when you cannot see the way ahead.

Endurance becomes possible when you trust that the journey is guided. Your strength is not just in what lies within you, it's in who walks ahead of you.

One woman said this verse became her personal anchor during a season of transition. "I didn't know what was coming," she said. "But I knew He was already there."

When you remember who goes before you, fear begins to fade.

Today, step forward with faith. Trust that the Lord has already gone ahead to prepare your way.

What does it mean to you that the Lord will never fail or forsake you?

September 30

> *"Let us hold fast the profession of our faith without wavering; (for he is faithful that promised;)"*
>
> Hebrews 10:23

To walk with Christ is to hold fast, not just to beliefs, but to hope. When life shakes your certainty, let your grip on Him tighten. When doubt whispers, hold on to the promises He has already fulfilled. He is faithful.

Enduring faith is not about never questioning. It is about trusting through the questions. And it's built on the character of a Savior who never breaks His word.

One brother said he kept a journal of answered prayers and spiritual moments. "When I started to doubt," he said, "I'd read those pages. They reminded me, He's been faithful before, and He will be again."

Faith holds on because Christ holds true.

Today, remember a promise the Lord has kept to you. Let that memory renew your confidence in Him.

What helps you hold fast to your faith when life feels uncertain?

October

**Build your life on the word of God
and let His truth guide every step.**

October 1

> *"Therefore whosoever heareth these sayings of mine, and doeth them, I will liken him unto a wise man, which built his house upon a rock:"*
> Matthew 7:24

THE SAVIOR TAUGHT THAT hearing and doing His word builds a foundation strong enough to withstand any storm. His teachings are not suggestions, they are anchors. When you build your life on His truth, you do not need to fear what comes.

This foundation is built through daily choices. Studying scripture. Following the counsel of prophets. Listening to personal revelation. These simple acts create spiritual strength that lasts.

One young adult shared, "There were moments when everything around me felt uncertain. But I never felt shaken. I knew what I believed, and I knew where to turn."

Building on Christ means trusting His words more than the world's opinions.

Today, recommit to building on the Savior's words. Let His truth become your daily anchor.

What are you doing each day to strengthen your foundation in Christ?

October 2

> *"For the word of God is quick, and powerful, and sharper than any twoedged sword, piercing even to the dividing asunder of soul and spirit, and of the joints and marrow, and is a discerner of the thoughts and intents of the heart."*
>
> Hebrews 4:12

Scripture is more than history. It is living truth. It has the power to pierce through confusion, lift discouragement, and give light to the path ahead. When you engage with the word of God, you invite power into your life.

That power is not just felt in grand revelations. It is felt in daily quiet moments when a verse speaks peace to your heart, or when a story reminds you of who you are.

One sister said, "Every time I return to the scriptures, I find something new. Not because the words changed, but because I did."

God's word meets you where you are and lifts you to where you can become.

Today, open your scriptures with the intent to hear God. Let His word speak directly to your heart.

When have the scriptures given you strength exactly when you needed it?

October 3

> *"What I the Lord have spoken, I have spoken, and I excuse not myself; and though the heavens and the earth pass away, my word shall not pass away, but shall all be fulfilled, whether by mine own voice or by the voice of my servants, it is the same."*
>
> Doctrine and Covenants 1:38

When prophets speak, the Lord is speaking. Their messages are not simply good advice, they are divine direction for our time. Listening to their words helps us align our lives with heaven.

In every general conference, there are specific messages meant just for you. As you listen with spiritual ears, the Holy Ghost will highlight what you need to hear, remember, and do.

One young man said, "Each time I listen, I hear something that feels personal. It's like God knows my thoughts and is answering them through His prophets."

The Lord continues to speak. And He speaks to you.

Today, reflect on a recent message from a prophet or apostle. Ask the Lord how He wants you to apply it.

How can you more intentionally listen for the Lord's voice through His chosen servants?

October 4

> *"... Wherefore, I said unto you, feast upon the words of Christ; for behold, the words of Christ will tell you all things what ye should do."*
> 2 Nephi 32:3

The word of God is meant to nourish your soul, not just inform your mind. When you feast on the scriptures—not just nibble or glance—you are filled with spiritual direction, strength, and peace.

The more you turn to the word, the more clearly you hear the voice of the Lord. His counsel becomes familiar, and His Spirit becomes your guide.

One woman said she began reading her scriptures with a question in her heart each day. "The answers didn't always come right away," she said, "but I always left with more light than I had before."

God's word feeds your faith. It fills you with what you need most.

Today, approach your scripture study as a spiritual feast. Come with hunger, and let the Lord fill you.

What does it mean to you to *feast* on the word of Christ, not just read it?

October 5

"We live in a world that is complex and increasingly contentious. The constant availability of social media and a 24-hour news cycle bombard us with relentless messages."

President Russell M. Nelson

With so many voices competing for your attention, it can be easy to feel overwhelmed. But one voice brings clarity above the noise, the voice of the Lord, often heard through His prophets and His word.

When you choose to quiet the world and focus on spiritual truth, you begin to hear peace again. You begin to feel what is right and know where to go.

One sister said she began limiting her screen time and replacing it with General Conference talks. "It changed everything," she said. "I felt more calm, more grounded. I felt God again."

What you focus on shapes how you feel. Focus on Him.

Today, quiet one voice of the world so you can better hear the voice of God. Let peace return.

What helps you tune out the noise and hear the Lord more clearly?

October 6

> *"And now, as the preaching of the word had a great tendency to lead the people to do that which was just—yea, it had had more powerful effect upon the minds of the people than the sword, or anything else, which had happened unto them—therefore Alma thought it was expedient that they should try the virtue of the word of God."*
>
> Alma 31:5

The word of God changes hearts more powerfully than force ever could. It teaches truth, invites repentance, and inspires righteousness. When we share and receive His word with humility, it begins to shape who we are.

That power is not limited to ancient scripture. It's also in modern prophetic counsel. God speaks today, and His word still transforms lives.

One brother shared that after returning to church, a single conference talk turned everything around for him. "It felt like the Lord was inviting me back personally," he said. "And I listened."

The word of God has power to reach deep into the soul and begin healing.

Today, let the word of God soften something in your heart. Trust in its power to change you.

What effect has the word of God had on your life lately?

October 7

"We can always trust the living prophets; their teachings reflect the word and will of the Lord. Surely the Lord God will do nothing, but he revealeth his secret unto his servants the prophets."

Elder José A. Teixeira

Trusting the prophets is an act of faith and a source of peace. Their counsel is not outdated or optional. It is current, clear, and centered in Christ. When you choose to follow it, you align yourself with heaven.

Prophetic counsel often provides direction before the need becomes obvious. It protects. It prepares. It strengthens. And it leads us closer to the Savior.

One young woman said, "When I started treating conference talks like scripture, everything changed. I began to hear the Lord's voice more clearly."

The more you listen, the more personal the counsel becomes.

Today, reread or relisten to one recent prophetic message. Ask the Lord what He wants you to do with it.

How has following prophetic counsel brought peace or clarity into your life?

October 8

> *"Open your mouths and they shall be filled, and you shall become even as Nephi of old, who journeyed from Jerusalem in the wilderness."*
>
> Doctrine and Covenants 33:8

God's word doesn't just fill hearts, it fills mouths. When you study the scriptures and heed the words of living prophets, you gain the language of faith. The Spirit brings truth to your remembrance when you need it most, often in moments of testimony, teaching, or comfort.

You may not feel eloquent or ready. But the Lord promises that when you open your mouth in faith, He will fill it with what matters.

One young missionary said, "I worried I wouldn't know what to say. But when I focused on what I had studied and trusted the Spirit, the words came. They always came."

The more you fill yourself with truth, the more you can share it.

Today, pray for the Spirit to help you speak words of truth and encouragement. Let God use your voice.

When has the Lord helped you speak or testify beyond your natural ability?

October 9

> *"We have been promised the constant companionship of the third member of the Godhead and hence the privilege of receiving revelation for our own lives."*
>
> Sister Sheri L. Dew

When you build your life on the word of God, you don't walk alone. The Holy Ghost becomes your constant companion, helping you discern truth, remember what matters, and apply the Lord's teachings in daily life.

Spiritual strength is not just about study, it's about companionship. The scriptures and prophetic counsel invite the Spirit. And the Spirit makes the truth personal, specific, and clear.

One sister said, "I started asking, 'What is the Spirit teaching me through this talk?' It changed the way I listened. Suddenly, the messages weren't just good, they were mine."

The Spirit is the teacher that makes truth stick.

Today, invite the Holy Ghost to teach you through scripture or a prophetic message. Write down what you feel.

How do you recognize when the Holy Ghost is helping you understand and apply God's word?

October 10

> "Behold, I speak unto all who have good desires, and have thrust in their sickle to reap."
> Doctrine and Covenants 11:27

The Lord speaks not just to prophets but to anyone with a willing heart and a desire to build His kingdom. If you want to be part of His work, He wants to speak to you. And He often does so through His word, written and spoken.

Scripture and modern revelation are not only for study. They are a call to action. They help you find your place in His work and prepare you to serve with power.

One brother said, "Every time I read the scriptures with a question in mind, I feel directed. It's like God is showing me how to help in His vineyard."

When you seek to serve, His word becomes your guide.

Today, ask the Lord what part of His work He wants you to focus on right now. Let the scriptures guide your answer.

How does your desire to serve the Lord help you receive more personal revelation?

October 11

> *"For it is God which worketh in you both to will and to do of his good pleasure."*
> Philippians 2:13

When you tune your heart to the voice of the Lord, you begin to recognize His influence in your daily life. You see His fingerprints in your blessings, in your learning, and in the gentle nudges of the Spirit.

The word of God trains your eyes to see and your ears to hear. As you reflect on what He is teaching you, through scripture and prophetic counsel, you begin to experience spiritual momentum.

One sister said, "The more I wrote down the spiritual things I noticed, the more I noticed. It was like God had been there all along. I just hadn't been looking."

Seeing God's hand builds faith, and faith opens your eyes even wider.

Today, look back on your week and write down where you have seen the Lord's hand. Give Him thanks.

What helps you recognize and remember the ways God is guiding and blessing you?

October 12

> *"Search the scriptures; for in them ye think ye have eternal life: and they are they which testify of me."*
>
> John 5:39

The scriptures are more than a collection of wise sayings or ancient stories. They are a living testimony of Jesus Christ. Every book, every verse, and every prophet points to Him. When you search the scriptures, you are seeking to know the Savior more personally.

The more you study His word, the more you begin to see Him, not just in the pages, but in your life. His mercy, His power, and His love become more real.

One man said, "I used to study the scriptures for answers. Now I study them to find Him. And when I find Him, I find everything else too."

The scriptures testify of Christ. And through them, you come to know Him.

Today, open your scriptures with a desire to see the Savior more clearly. Let your study deepen your relationship with Him.

How have the scriptures helped you come to know Jesus Christ more personally?

October 13

"As you bear testimony of what you know, believe, and feel, the Holy Ghost will confirm the truth to those who earnestly listen to your testimony."

Elder M. Russell Ballard

Listening to prophets is not just about hearing their words. It is about believing that God is speaking through them, and then acting on what you hear. When you combine their counsel with faith, the Holy Ghost confirms truth and inspires change.

Sometimes the change is immediate. Other times it comes gradually, as you live with intention and keep returning to their messages.

One sister shared, "I started reviewing just one quote from conference each day. It helped me stay focused on the Spirit all week long."

The words of prophets carry power because they point us to the Savior.

Today, choose one piece of prophetic counsel to focus on. Write it down and act on it with faith.

How do you keep the messages from living prophets in your heart after conference ends?

October 14

> *"For behold, did not Moses prophesy unto them concerning the coming of the Messiah, and that God should redeem his people? Yea, and even all the prophets who have prophesied ever since the world began—have they not spoken more or less concerning these things?"*
> Mosiah 13:33

From the beginning, prophets have pointed the world to Jesus Christ. Their role has always been to prepare hearts, correct course, and remind us of the Savior's redeeming love. Their voices echo across time with one unchanging message: *come unto Christ.*

When you study their words—ancient or modern—you are connecting with that same invitation. You are aligning your life with divine purpose.

One man said, "When I read from the Book of Mormon and listen to General Conference, I feel like I'm standing in the same place spiritually, right at the feet of the Lord's servants."

Every prophetic voice points to Christ. And He is always the center.

Today, read one testimony of Christ from a prophet, ancient or modern. Let it strengthen your own.

How do the testimonies of prophets help you feel closer to the Savior?

October 15

> *"The words of the Lord are pure words: as silver tried in a furnace of earth, purified seven times."*
>
> Psalm 12:6

God's words are not ordinary. They are refined, purposeful, and eternal. They cut through confusion, calm the heart, and invite change. When you let His words dwell in you, they shape who you are becoming.

Whether through scripture, prophetic teaching, or personal revelation, the Lord's words are clear and trustworthy. They guide you to safety and fill you with peace.

One sister said, "I started writing down any verse or phrase that stood out to me each day. Over time, those words became a source of comfort I could always return to."

God's word doesn't just inform. It transforms.

Today, treasure one line of scripture or counsel. Let it stay with you and speak to your heart throughout the day.

What helps you hold onto the words the Lord speaks to you personally?

October 16

> *"Behold, I will hasten my work in its time."*
> Doctrine and Covenants 88:73

God's work moves forward on His timeline, but it moves with purpose and power. When we listen to the voice of modern prophets, we hear how the Lord is hastening His work and inviting us to be part of it. Their words help us see the bigger picture and understand where we fit.

Sometimes the pace feels fast. Other times, it feels like we are just preparing. But when we trust His timing and follow His voice, we are always in the right place at the right time.

One man said, "I used to feel like I was behind in my spiritual journey. But when I focused on following the prophet, I realized I was right where I needed to be."

The Lord will hasten His work, and He will do it through His people.

Today, ask the Lord how you can be part of His work. Listen for His direction through scripture or prophetic counsel.

What helps you stay in step with the Lord's pace as He moves His work forward?

October 17

> *"And he gave some, apostles; and some, prophets; and some, evangelists; and some, pastors and teachers; For the perfecting of the saints, for the work of the ministry, for the edifying of the body of Christ:"*
> Ephesians 4:11–12

Prophets are a gift. They are given not to replace our personal revelation, but to enhance it, to lift, strengthen, and unify the body of Christ. Their words clarify doctrine, call us to repentance, and help us become more like the Savior.

When you take their words seriously, you feel spiritually safer. Their messages bring clarity in confusion and direction in uncertainty.

One sister said, "After conference, I felt like I had a spiritual map. I knew what to do next. I didn't feel lost anymore."

Prophets do not speak for themselves. They speak for the Lord.

Today, review one prophetic message and ask how it applies to your life. Let it guide your next step.

How does following the prophets strengthen your personal testimony and sense of purpose?

October 18

> *"And now, my sons, remember, remember that it is upon the rock of our Redeemer, who is Christ, the Son of God, that ye must build your foundation; ..."*
>
> Helaman 5:12

The world will always shift and shake, but the Savior is steady. Building your life on His word means building on something unmovable. When the foundation is Christ, everything else, including your identity, your choices, and your peace can stand firm.

His word is the blueprint for spiritual stability. Each time you read a verse, follow a prompting, or apply prophetic counsel, you add strength to your foundation.

One brother said, "When I started seeing my scripture study as foundation-building instead of just a habit, it became more sacred, and more powerful."

Foundations are built one choice at a time. And Christ is the rock that never crumbles.

Today, choose one small way to strengthen your spiritual foundation. Let it bring peace and steadiness.

What helps you build your life more intentionally on the foundation of Christ?

October 19

> *"Also I set watchmen over you, saying, Hearken to the sound of the trumpet. But they said, We will not hearken."*
>
> Jeremiah 6:17

When life feels uncertain, the Lord does not leave you to figure it out alone. He gives you guides through his prophets, apostles, and inspired leaders. These guides know the way back to Him. As you stay close to their teachings, you stay on safe paths.

Spiritual safety is not found in having all the answers. It's found in knowing where to turn and who to trust.

One woman said, "The more I listened to the prophet, the more confident I felt, even when life didn't look how I expected."

You don't have to navigate life alone. Stay close to those who know the way back to Christ.

Today, review a quote from our living prophet. Let it steady your steps and strengthen your direction.

Who has helped guide you spiritually, and how can you follow their example in your own life?

October 20

> *"For behold, again I say unto you that if ye will enter in by the way, and receive the Holy Ghost, it will show unto you all things what ye should do."*
>
> 2 Nephi 32:5

As you read scripture and listen to prophets, the Holy Ghost is the one who helps you understand, apply, and act. Revelation isn't just about information, it's about transformation. The Spirit personalizes truth, so you can know how to live it.

Sometimes the message will be direct. Other times, it will come as a quiet impression or a thought that settles in your heart. The key is to keep listening and keep trusting.

One brother shared, "I started asking after every talk or scripture, 'What does God want me to do about this?' The answers always came."

The Holy Ghost is your teacher and your guide. Let Him help you live the truth you receive.

Today, ask the Spirit to teach you what to do with a truth you've learned recently. Be willing to act on it.

What has the Holy Ghost taught you as you've studied scripture or prophetic words?

October 21

"The adversary is clever. For millennia he has been making good look evil and evil look good. His messages tend to be loud, bold, and boastful."

President Russell M. Nelson

The world is filled with messages that distort truth. Some sound appealing or popular, but they lead away from peace and purpose. In contrast, the Lord's voice is steady and clear. It calls you toward righteousness, compassion, and discipleship.

Prophets help us see clearly when the world tries to blur the lines. Their counsel may be bold, but it is never boastful. It is filled with love and centered on Christ.

One brother said, "I used to feel confused about what was right. But when I listened to the prophet, the confusion cleared. I knew who to trust."

The truth may not always be loud, but it is always powerful.

Today, reflect on one truth you've learned that goes against the world's message. Choose to follow it with faith.

How has prophetic counsel helped you see through the noise of the world?

October 22

> *"And by the power of the Holy Ghost ye may know the truth of all things."*
>
> Moroni 10:5

Truth is not always found in popularity or persuasion. It is confirmed by the Spirit. When you study the scriptures, listen to prophetic counsel, or seek personal answers, the Holy Ghost is the one who testifies to your heart that it is true.

This confirmation brings peace, not pressure. It creates clarity in confusion and confidence in your choices.

One young woman shared, "I was praying about a decision, and after reading my scriptures, I felt a quiet assurance I hadn't felt before. It didn't come with fireworks, just a calm *yes*."

Truth accompanied by the Spirit brings lasting peace.

Today, seek the Holy Ghost as you study or pray. Ask Him to confirm truth to your heart.

What does it feel like when the Spirit confirms something is true to you?

October 23

"I have long believed that the study of the doctrines of the gospel will improve behavior quicker than talking about behavior will improve behavior."

Elder Boyd K. Packer

Change that lasts doesn't begin with willpower. It begins with truth. When you study gospel doctrine and let the Lord's word enter your heart, it changes your desires, and changed desires lead to changed lives.

That's why consistent study matters. Not just to check a box, but to reshape your thinking, your choices, and your relationships. The more you understand God's doctrine, the more you understand yourself and your purpose.

One brother said, "When I was struggling, I started reading about Christ's attributes. It helped me not just act differently, but it helped me want different things."

God's word doesn't just correct. It transforms.

Today, study one doctrine that challenges or inspires you. Let it guide a new action.

What doctrine has helped shape your choices or desires for the better?

October 24

> "And I do this that I may prove unto many that I am the same yesterday, today, and forever; and that I speak forth my words according to mine own pleasure. And because that I have spoken one word ye need not suppose that I cannot speak another; for my work is not yet finished; neither shall it be until the end of man, neither from that time henceforth and forever."
>
> 2 Nephi 29:9

God's word is certain. It does not shift with time or opinion. What He promises, He fulfills. When you build your faith on the scriptures and the teachings of living prophets, you are anchoring your soul to something eternal.

This brings calm in a world that is constantly changing. When everything else feels uncertain, His word remains.

One woman said, "During a time when I didn't know who or what to trust, I kept coming back to the scriptures. They were the one place I always felt peace."

The Lord does not speak just to be heard. He speaks to be trusted.

Today, read one of God's promises in scripture and write how you've seen it fulfilled in your life.

What helps you trust that the Lord's words will always come to pass?

October 25

> *"But be ye doers of the word, and not hearers only, deceiving your own selves."*
>
> James 1:22

The power of God's word is not fully realized until it becomes part of your life. Scripture and prophetic counsel are meant to shape your actions, your priorities, and your relationships. They are not just truths to admire, but truths to apply.

Discipleship is about alignment by bringing your choices into harmony with God's voice.

One man shared, "I started asking each morning, 'What's one teaching I can live today?' It changed how I approached everything."

Living the word brings joy. It turns knowledge into transformation.

Today, choose one gospel principle to live more intentionally. Watch how it changes your day.

> **What truth have you recently learned that you're ready to start living more fully?**

October 26

> *"And now, behold, is your knowledge perfect? Yea, your knowledge is perfect in that thing, and your faith is dormant; and this because you know, for ye know that the word hath swelled your souls, and ye also know that it hath sprouted up, that your understanding doth begin to be enlightened, and your mind doth begin to expand."*
>
> Alma 32:34

Spiritual understanding often begins as a seed. You may not have all the answers, but when you act on the light you have, your faith begins to grow. Studying scripture and following prophetic counsel is part of that experiment of faith. Over time, the truth becomes more clear.

The Lord doesn't expect you to know everything now. He simply asks you to begin. As you nurture what you learn, your testimony deepens.

One sister shared, "At first, I wasn't sure about a principle I heard in conference. But I tried to live it, and slowly, it started to make sense. I felt the Spirit confirm it."

Faith grows through experience with truth.

Today, act on something you've learned, even if your testimony of it is still growing. Let the Lord enlighten you.

What small spiritual experiment has helped grow your understanding or faith?

October 27

"A prophet does not stand between you and the Savior. Rather, he stands beside you and points the way to the Savior."
                    Elder Neil L. Andersen

Every message from a prophet points to the Savior. Whether it's about repentance, service, the family, or faith, the end goal is always the same, to bring us closer to Jesus Christ. That is how you know their words are from God.

Prophetic counsel is not just about caution. It is about connection. When you listen, you begin to see Christ more clearly and understand what He desires for you.

One young man said, "I started listening to conference with one question: 'How is this leading me to Christ?' The answers always came."

The voice of the prophet is a guide to the heart of the Savior.

Today, revisit a recent talk and ask yourself how it brings you closer to Christ. Let it draw you nearer.

How have the prophets helped you strengthen your personal relationship with the Savior?

October 28

> *"And the light which shineth, which giveth you light, is through him who enlighteneth your eyes, which is the same light that quickeneth your understandings;"*
> Doctrine and Covenants 88:11

The light of Christ is found in many places, such as scripture, prophetic messages, prayer, and quiet reflection. That light doesn't just illuminate your path. It opens your understanding and helps you see yourself and others more clearly.

When you regularly seek light through His word, your spiritual eyes adjust. You begin to see truth in everyday moments and feel peace in difficult places.

One woman said, "There was a verse I'd read many times, but one day it suddenly meant something deeply personal. I knew it was the Lord opening my eyes."

Light from the Lord is personal. It brings clarity, comfort, and direction.

Today, ask the Lord to open your eyes to something new in His word. Be ready for light to shine.

When have you seen the Lord enlighten your understanding through scripture or prophetic teaching?

October 29

"We believe in a God who is engaged in our lives, who is not silent, ..."
Elder Jeffrey R. Holland

Sometimes the world can feel loud, and heaven can seem quiet. But the Lord is still speaking. He speaks through scripture, prophets, the Holy Ghost, and personal revelation. The question is not whether He is speaking, it is whether we are listening.

As you make space for His word, you begin to recognize His voice. It may come as peace, prompting, or sudden understanding. But it will come.

One young woman said, "I used to wonder why God wasn't talking to me. Then I realized I wasn't really listening. When I started paying attention, He had a lot to say."

God's silence is never distance. Often, it's an invitation to draw closer.

Today, spend a few quiet minutes with the Lord. Ask Him to speak, and listen with your heart.

What helps you recognize the ways God is speaking to you today?

October 30

> *"If any of you lack wisdom, let him ask of God, that giveth to all men liberally, and upbraideth not; and it shall be given him."*
>
> James 1:5

This single verse changed the course of history. It also changes individual lives. God invites questions. He welcomes your seeking. And through scripture, prophets, and the Holy Ghost, He answers with love and clarity.

The promise isn't just for Joseph Smith. It's for you. Every time you sincerely ask, the Lord responds, maybe not all at once, but always in a way that blesses you.

One brother shared, "When I didn't understand a gospel principle, I prayed and then studied. The answer came in pieces, but it came. And it was exactly what I needed."

Questions are not signs of weakness. They are invitations to receive revelation.

Today, ask the Lord a question that's been on your heart. Then listen, study, and trust He will answer.

What questions have led you to deeper understanding and stronger faith?

October 31

> *"And we talk of Christ, we rejoice in Christ, we preach of Christ, we prophesy of Christ, and we write according to our prophecies, that our children may know to what source they may look for a remission of their sins."*
>
> 2 Nephi 25:26

Everything in the gospel points to Jesus Christ. Every prophet, every scripture, every prompting leads back to Him. As you build your life on His word, you build your life on the One who never fails.

Christ is not just the center of our doctrine, He is the center of our hope. His words offer healing, His example shows the way, and His love gives us the strength to endure.

One sister said, "When I started to really focus on Christ in everything—my study, my prayers, my decisions—everything else started to fall into place."

Make Him your foundation, your message, and your joy.

Today, rejoice in Christ. Let your thoughts, your study, and your choices center on Him.

How can you more fully place Christ at the center of your study, worship, and daily life?

November

Choose gratitude in Christ and discover joy, peace, and contentment in every season.

November 1

> *"O give thanks unto the Lord, for he is good:*
> *for his mercy endureth for ever."*
>
> Psalm 107:1

GRATITUDE BEGINS WITH REMEMBERING who God is. He is good. He is merciful. He is constant. When we focus on His character and reflect on His blessings, gratitude begins to grow. Not just in response to blessings, but as a way of seeing.

True gratitude is more than a list. It is a lens. It changes how you view your challenges, your blessings, and your daily life. It softens the heart and opens the door for more joy.

One woman shared, "When I started my prayers with thanks instead of requests, my whole mindset shifted. I felt more peace, even when life was hard."

Gratitude helps you see the goodness of God in every season.

Today, begin your prayers with five things you're grateful for. Let it set the tone for your day.

What happens when you start your day by giving thanks to the Lord?

November 2

> *"And he who receiveth all things with thankfulness shall be made glorious; and the things of this earth shall be added unto him, even an hundred fold, yea, more."*
> Doctrine and Covenants 78:19

Receiving with thankfulness is not about pretending everything is perfect. It is about welcoming both blessings and lessons with a heart that trusts in God's plan. This kind of gratitude transforms not only how you feel, but who you become.

The promise is clear. When you choose gratitude, glory follows. That glory might not be immediate or visible, but it is spiritual. It brings light to your soul and strength to your testimony.

One young woman said, "I started keeping a gratitude journal, and it helped me see how much God was doing, even in small ways. It made me feel closer to Him."

Gratitude unlocks joy and deepens your connection with heaven.

Today, write down three moments from the past week that you are thankful for. Reflect on how they brought you closer to Christ.

How has choosing to receive life with thankfulness changed your perspective?

November 3

"Count your many blessings; name them one by one, And it will surprise you what the Lord has done."
    Count Your Blessings, Hymns, no. 241

Gratitude has a way of opening our eyes. When we take time to name our blessings, we begin to realize how present the Lord has been all along. What once felt ordinary becomes sacred. What once seemed small becomes evidence of His care.

Counting blessings is more than a spiritual exercise. It is a way to build faith. Each remembered blessing becomes a stepping stone that helps us move forward with greater trust.

One brother said, "I started keeping a list on my phone. Any time something good happened, I added it. Looking back, it's helped me see God's hand even during hard times."

Even the smallest blessings are worth noticing.

Today, list five blessings you may have overlooked recently. Let them remind you of the Lord's presence.

What helps you stay aware of God's hand in your daily life?

November 4

> *"And upon these I write the things of my soul, and many of the scriptures which are engraven upon the plates of brass. For my soul delighteth in the scriptures, and my heart pondereth them, and writeth them for the learning and the profit of my children."*
>
> 2 Nephi 4:15

Joy is not just found in comfort or ease. It is found in the things of the Lord. His word, His grace, His mercy, and His love. When your soul begins to delight in Him, you begin to feel joy that is steady, lasting, and full of light.

Gratitude and joy are deeply connected. As you thank the Lord for His goodness, your capacity to feel joy grows. That joy becomes more resilient than momentary happiness. It becomes a spiritual strength.

One young woman said, "The more I looked for the Lord in my life, the more joy I found. Not because things got easier, but because I knew He was with me."

Joy rooted in Christ cannot be shaken.

Today, look for one moment that brings you joy in the Lord. Write it down and give thanks for it.

How can you cultivate more joy by focusing on the things of the Lord?

November 5

> *"In every thing give thanks: for this is the will of God in Christ Jesus concerning you."*
> 1 Thessalonians 5:18

Giving thanks in everything does not mean everything will feel good. It means choosing to find gratitude even when life feels uncertain. It is about turning your heart toward heaven in all things, not just in success, but in struggle.

This kind of gratitude is powerful. It turns ordinary days into sacred experiences. It reminds you that God is at work, even in the hard moments.

One sister said, "I began thanking God not just for blessings, but for what I was learning. It didn't change the situation, but it changed me."

Gratitude does not require perfection. It invites perspective.

Today, offer thanks in a situation that still feels unresolved. Trust that the Lord is working through it.

What helps you give thanks in all things, not just when life is easy?

November 6

> *"Yea, they did cry: Hosanna to the Most High God. And they did cry: Blessed be the name of the Lord God Almighty, the Most High God."*
> 3 Nephi 4:32

Gratitude naturally flows into praise. When your heart is full of thanks, your spirit wants to rejoice. Singing praises, offering prayers, or simply expressing joy is a way to honor the Giver of all good things. Praise is more than a song, it is a spiritual response, a way of turning the soul upward in reverence and love.

The more you praise, the more you feel joy. Praise helps lift burdens and deepen your trust. It shifts your focus from what you lack to what the Lord has already done. It helps you see how present He has been in every step, how near He remains, and how perfectly He provides.

One brother said, "On hard days, I try to thank God out loud for one thing. It lifts the weight a little every time." That small act of vocal gratitude often unlocks a deeper peace, one that carries you through the hard moments with hope.

Praise is the overflow of a grateful heart. It transforms your perspective and deepens your connection to heaven.

Today, speak your gratitude out loud to the Lord. Let it turn into praise.

What does it feel like when gratitude leads you to rejoice in the Lord?

November 7

> *"And let my servant Edward Partridge stand in the office to which I have appointed him, and divide unto the saints their inheritance, even as I have commanded; and also those whom he has appointed to assist him."*
> Doctrine and Covenants 59:7

This commandment is not about politeness. It is about perspective. Gratitude in all things brings the Spirit into your life. It helps you recognize the Lord's hand and remember that you are never alone in your journey.

Thanking God in all things requires faith. It means trusting that He is working for your good, even when blessings come in unexpected ways.

One woman said, "I began thanking the Lord even during my trials. It didn't make the pain go away, but it gave me peace. It reminded me that He was still with me."

Gratitude brings you closer to God, no matter your circumstances.

Today, find something to be thankful for in a situation that feels difficult. Let it shift your focus.

How does expressing gratitude in trials bring you closer to the Savior?

November 8

> *"The thankful heart opens our eyes to a multitude of blessings that continually surround us."*
> President Thomas S. Monson

Sometimes we overlook blessings because we are focused on what we lack. A thankful heart changes that. It helps us see what we already have and recognize the daily miracles the Lord places in our path. Gratitude does not require a perfect life, just a willing heart. One that pauses long enough to notice the quiet ways God is showing up.

Gratitude turns your attention outward. It invites humility and joy. It teaches your soul to see through a spiritual lens, one that finds beauty in the ordinary and peace in the present moment. When you are truly thankful, you see the abundance of God's goodness, even in small things.

One young man said, "When I started looking for things to be grateful for each day, I was shocked at how many there were. It changed how I saw my life."

Blessings multiply when you learn to see them. A thankful heart doesn't wait for more, it rejoices in what is already there.

Today, look around and name three small blessings you would usually overlook. Let them lift your heart.

What are some ordinary things that bring extraordinary joy when you stop to notice them?

November 9

"And let the peace of God rule in your hearts, to the which also ye are called in one body; and be ye thankful."

Colossians 3:15

Gratitude invites peace. When you choose to give thanks, even in uncertainty, your heart becomes more open to the calming influence of the Spirit. Peace is not just the absence of problems. It is the presence of God, made clearer through a thankful heart.

Gratitude softens your reactions and settles your spirit. It makes room for contentment, even when your circumstances have not yet changed.

One sister shared, "When I started praying with more thanks than requests, I felt more peace. Not because everything was solved, but because I felt closer to the Lord."

Peace grows where gratitude is planted.

Today, express gratitude in prayer before asking for anything. Let it prepare your heart for peace.

How does thankfulness change the way you feel about your current situation?

November 10

> *"Gratitude is a catalyst to all Christlike attributes! A thankful heart is the parent of all virtues."*
>
> Elder Dieter F. Uchtdorf

Gratitude strengthens everything else. It nurtures humility, builds patience, and inspires generosity. When you are truly thankful, you begin to see others more clearly and serve them more willingly. Your discipleship deepens.

It is no surprise that gratitude is described as a saving principle. It connects you to Christ and reflects His light. It helps you become more like Him in both heart and habit.

One brother said, "When I started focusing on gratitude, my frustrations shrank. I became more patient and more willing to forgive. I realized that when I was constantly dwelling on what was wrong, it was hard to see anything good. But as I chose to thank God for even the little things, it softened my heart. I found myself letting go of grudges faster and seeing people with more compassion."

Gratitude is not just a response to blessings. It is a way of becoming more Christlike.

Today, reflect on how gratitude is shaping your character. Thank the Lord for the growth you are seeing.

Which Christlike qualities are you developing more fully because of a thankful heart?

November 11

> *"And they have brought forth children; yea, even the family of all the earth."*
>
> 2 Nephi 2:20

Prospering in the Lord's eyes does not always mean material success. It often means peace of conscience, joy in daily living, and strength through trials. These are the quiet, sacred blessings that come from walking in obedience and expressing gratitude.

When you recognize prosperity in spiritual terms, you begin to see the richness of your life in new ways. Obedience and gratitude work together to unlock deeper happiness.

One sister said, "As I focused more on what I had than what I wanted, I realized how spiritually full my life already was."

Gratitude makes you aware of the prosperity God is already giving you.

Today, thank the Lord for a spiritual blessing you may have taken for granted. Let it deepen your joy.

What does it mean to you to prosper in the Lord's way?

November 12

> *"And he who receiveth all things with thankfulness shall be made glorious; and the things of this earth shall be added unto him, even an hundred fold, yea, more."*
> Doctrine and Covenants 78:19

Thankfulness transforms how you receive life. It does not mean pretending everything is easy. It means trusting that even in difficulty, God is with you. That trust brings light, and that light brings glory.

Glory may not come as recognition or ease. It may come as quiet strength, increased compassion, or a heart filled with hope. These are the fruits of a soul that receives life with gratitude.

One sister said, "Gratitude didn't fix my problems. But it helped me feel God in the middle of them. That changed everything."

Gratitude prepares you for spiritual glory by opening your heart to the light of Christ.

Today, receive this day with thankfulness, no matter what it brings. Trust the Lord to make it meaningful.

How does receiving your life with gratitude change the way you experience it?

November 13

> *"And now behold, I say unto you, my brethren, if ye have experienced a change of heart, and if ye have felt to sing the song of redeeming love, I would ask, can ye feel so now?"*
>
> Alma 5:26

Gratitude is closely tied to remembrance. When you recall the moments the Savior changed your heart or lifted your burdens, your spirit fills with love again. The feeling to "sing the song of redeeming love" is a reminder to recognize His hand in your life right now.

You don't need a dramatic story to feel this joy. Sometimes it's simply feeling peace after prayer, or strength in the middle of the day. These are sacred moments worth noticing.

One sister shared, "When I take time to remember how the Lord has helped me, I can feel that gratitude again. It reconnects me with Him."

Gratitude grows as you remember how Christ has walked with you.

Today, write down one way the Lord has helped you change or grow. Give thanks for that transformation.

How can remembering your spiritual milestones deepen your gratitude today?

November 14

> *"Rejoice evermore. Pray without ceasing. In every thing give thanks: for this is the will of God in Christ Jesus concerning you."*
> 1 Thessalonians 5:16–18

These short instructions from Paul carry deep power. Rejoicing, praying, and giving thanks are not just reactions, they are choices. They are habits that shape your heart and bring you closer to Christ.

Gratitude strengthens your prayer life and magnifies your ability to rejoice. When you pray with a thankful heart, your burdens feel lighter. When you rejoice in small things, you begin to notice more of them.

One young man said, "My prayers used to feel routine. Then I started thanking God for specifics. I noticed more joy and more connection."

Spiritual habits rooted in gratitude bring lasting happiness.

Today, pray with only gratitude. Rejoice in what the Lord has already done. Let it shape your day.

What spiritual habits help you stay grounded in joy and thanksgiving?

November 15

> *"When thou hast eaten and art full, then thou shalt bless the Lord thy God for the good land which he hath given thee."*
>
> Deuteronomy 8:10

Gratitude invites you to pause and recognize not just what God has done, but where He has placed you. Your circumstances, relationships, and even your trials are part of the ground He has given you to grow in.

It is easy to focus on where you want to be next. But today's blessings deserve to be named. When you bless the Lord for the good land you have now, your eyes open to the richness already around you.

One sister said, "I used to pray for things to change. Then I started praying with gratitude for what already was. It brought contentment I hadn't felt before."

Thanksgiving turns your current place into sacred ground.

Today, offer thanks for the season of life you're in right now, even if it's imperfect. Let it soften your heart.

What in your life right now deserves more gratitude than you've been giving it?

November 16

"Gratitude is a divine principle."
President Thomas S. Monson

Gratitude is not only polite. It is powerful. It has the ability to change the atmosphere of your heart and invite blessings that might not come otherwise. When you express true thanks, you are aligning your heart with heaven.

The windows of heaven open not just with material blessings, but with revelation, peace, and joy. These spiritual gifts often come quietly, but they come more readily when our hearts are prepared to receive them. Gratitude clears that space. It shifts our focus, quiets our complaints, and helps us become more aware of the divine help already surrounding us. When we are grateful, we are more likely to recognize the Spirit's whisper, the reassurance in a quiet moment, or the guidance tucked inside an ordinary day.

One brother shared, "I was struggling with a decision. When I prayed with gratitude first, I felt more clarity. I believe the gratitude opened my heart to receive the Lord's direction."

Heaven responds to a thankful heart.

Today, express gratitude for a recent answer to prayer or spiritual prompting. Let it build your faith.

How has gratitude helped open spiritual doors in your life?

November 17

> *"And now, my sons, remember, remember that it is upon the rock of our Redeemer, who is Christ, the Son of God, that ye must build your foundation;..."*
>
> Helaman 5:12

Gratitude becomes deeper when it is built on the foundation of Christ. It is more than being thankful for things, it becomes a recognition of who He is and what He has done. Gratitude rooted in the Savior brings lasting strength and unshakable peace.

When trials come, that foundation holds. When blessings arrive, it brings even more praise. With Christ as the center, your gratitude gains eternal perspective.

One woman shared, "I realized that when I was grateful for Christ Himself—not just what He did for me—I felt more joy and less fear."

Christ is not just the source of blessings. He is the greatest blessing.

Today, focus your gratitude on the Savior. Thank Him not only for what He gives, but for who He is.

How does your foundation in Christ shape your expression of gratitude?

November 18

> *"Gratitude is the beginning of civility, of decency and goodness, of a recognition that we cannot afford to be arrogant. We should walk with the knowledge that we will need help every step of the way."*
> President Gordon B. Hinckley

A thankful heart is often the beginning of many other virtues. It leads to kindness, humility, reverence, and love. It helps you treat others and yourself with more patience and compassion. Gratitude expands the soul.

When you live with thanksgiving, your attitude becomes gentler and your perspective becomes more eternal. You start to see with spiritual eyes.

One sister said, "When I focused more on being thankful, I found myself speaking more gently, feeling more hope, and remembering the Lord more often."

Gratitude is not just an act. It is a way of living that shapes your spirit.

Today, notice how gratitude changes your behavior. Let it inspire more kindness and humility.

What other Christlike attributes grow stronger when you begin with gratitude?

November 19

> *"O generation of vipers, how can ye, being evil, speak good things? for out of the abundance of the heart the mouth speaketh."*
>
> Matthew 12:34

What fills your heart will eventually shape your words. When your heart is full of gratitude, your conversations begin to reflect it. You speak with more kindness, more hope, and more reverence for what the Lord is doing in your life.

Gratitude expressed aloud blesses others. It encourages them, lifts their burdens, and points their hearts to God. It also reinforces your own testimony as you speak truth and light into your day.

One brother said, "When I started voicing gratitude out loud—even for little things—I noticed more joy in my home. It changed the atmosphere."

Gratitude that lives in your heart is powerful. Gratitude that is spoken becomes a blessing to others.

Today, express gratitude aloud to someone you love. Let your words lift and encourage.

What can you say today that reflects a grateful heart?

November 20

> *"And ye must give thanks unto God in the Spirit for whatsoever blessing ye are blessed with."*
>
> Doctrine and Covenants 46:32

Some blessings are easy to recognize. Others are quiet, unexpected, or disguised in trial. Giving thanks in the Spirit means inviting the Holy Ghost to help you see what God is doing, even when it's not obvious.

The Spirit expands your awareness. It helps you notice grace where you once saw inconvenience, and miracles where you once felt overwhelmed.

One young woman said, "I started praying for help to see the blessings I was missing. That simple prayer helped me notice more, and thank God more."

Spiritual gratitude is not based on circumstances. It's based on revelation.

Today, ask the Holy Ghost to help you see a hidden blessing. Thank God for what He reveals.

How does the Spirit help you become more aware of the Lord's goodness?

November 21

> *"Thanks be unto God for his unspeakable gift."*
>
> 2 Corinthians 9:15

The greatest gift you have ever received is Jesus Christ. His life, His atoning sacrifice, His resurrection, and His grace are the foundation of every other blessing. Gratitude becomes more sacred when it flows from this recognition.

Thanking God for Christ transforms your perspective. It centers your heart, even when life feels unsteady. It reminds you that your hope is not based on circumstances, but on eternal truth.

One sister shared, "When I was struggling to feel thankful, I focused on the Savior. Just remembering Him brought peace to my heart." She explained that during a particularly hard season, everything felt overwhelming and blessings seemed hard to see. But as she studied the scriptures and reflected on the Savior's love, she began to notice moments of comfort that had been there all along. "He had not taken away my trial," she said, "but He had carried me through it in ways I hadn't realized until I started looking for Him."

Christ is the reason we can feel joy in every season.

Today, offer a prayer of thanks focused only on Jesus Christ. Let your gratitude deepen your love for Him.

What specific gift from the Savior are you most thankful for right now?

November 22

> "That ye contend no more against the Holy Ghost, but that ye receive it, and take upon you the name of Christ; that ye humble yourselves even to the dust, and worship God, in whatsoever place ye may be in, in spirit and in truth; and that ye live in thanksgiving daily, for the many mercies and blessings which he doth bestow upon you."
>
> Alma 34:38

Daily thanksgiving is more than a holiday tradition. It is a way of living that brings heaven into your ordinary routine. When you choose to thank the Lord every day, your life becomes a reflection of His goodness.

This habit of gratitude does not require dramatic blessings. It simply requires awareness. Small acts of grace, a kind word, a peaceful moment, each one is evidence of God's love.

One young man said, "I put a sticky note on my mirror that says 'Thank God for one thing.' It's a simple reminder, but it helps me live more joyfully."

Daily gratitude invites daily joy.

Today, start a small daily gratitude ritual. Keep it simple, but keep it consistent.

What helps you live in thanksgiving every day, not just once in a while?

November 23

> *"Enter into his gates with thanksgiving, and into his courts with praise: be thankful unto him, and bless his name."*
>
> Psalm 100:4

Thanksgiving is more than a polite response. It is the way we come closer to God. When we approach Him with gratitude, we enter holy space. Our hearts become more prepared to receive His Spirit, His guidance, and His peace. Gratitude is not just an emotional reaction, it is a spiritual practice that invites the presence of the Lord.

This kind of thankfulness is an act of worship. It shifts our focus from what we lack to who He is. It reorients our desires and reminds us that God Himself is our greatest gift. When we thank Him for His character, His mercy, patience, and goodness, we are drawn into deeper reverence.

One sister shared, "When I began treating gratitude like a form of worship, not just a feeling, I felt the Spirit more deeply in my life."

Gratitude opens the door to deeper communion with God. It makes ordinary prayers sacred. It turns everyday moments into encounters with divine love.

Today, make your prayer a form of worship. Praise the Lord and thank Him for who He is.

How does gratitude change the way you approach the Lord in prayer and worship?

November 24

> *"Gratitude is the memory of the heart."*
> Jean-Baptiste Massieu, often quoted by
> President Thomas S. Monson

To be truly grateful is to remember. It is to carry blessings not just in your mind, but in your heart. Remembering what the Lord has done helps you trust what He is doing and believe in what He will yet do.

When you pause to remember, your heart becomes more grounded in peace and anchored in faith.

One young adult said, "I keep a small journal of spiritual moments. On hard days, I go back and remember. That habit keeps me hopeful."

Memory fuels gratitude. And gratitude builds spiritual confidence.

Today, reflect on a time when the Lord helped you. Let it renew your trust in Him today.

What blessings from your past still shape your faith in the present?

November 25

> *"He revealeth the deep and secret things: he knoweth what is in the darkness, and the light dwelleth with him."*
>
> Daniel 2:22

Some blessings are easy to notice. Others require the Spirit to reveal them. Giving thanks in the Spirit means being spiritually aware of how God is working in your life. It means looking beyond the surface and recognizing His quiet miracles.

When your heart is tuned to the Spirit, you begin to notice the subtle and sacred ways God is working in your life. Gratitude deepens as your spiritual vision sharpens, revealing blessings that once seemed hidden or ordinary, but now feel profoundly personal and divine.

One sister said, "I used to thank God only for the obvious. Then I started asking the Spirit to help me see what I was missing. It changed the way I prayed."

Spiritual gratitude sees the invisible and celebrates the eternal.

Today, ask the Spirit to show you one hidden blessing you might have missed. Thank the Lord for it.

How has the Holy Ghost helped you notice the quiet, personal blessings in your life?

November 26

> *"The Lord hath done great things for us; whereof we are glad."*
>
> Psalm 126:3

Sometimes it is good to stop and say it plainly, *the Lord has done great things*. Your life is filled with evidence of His goodness, His mercy, and His power. Acknowledging that truth brings light to your soul and deepens your joy.

This kind of gratitude is not about pretending everything is perfect. It is about choosing to see the fingerprints of God, even in imperfect moments.

One young man shared, "When I'm discouraged, I say this verse out loud. It reminds me of who I'm walking with."

The blessings bestowed upon us by God are not always immediately apparent or outwardly dramatic in their manifestation. Sometimes they look like peace, people, or quiet strength.

Today, write a simple statement: "The Lord has done great things for me." List three of them.

How does remembering the Lord's greatness help you feel more joy and peace today?

November 27

> "Counsel with the Lord in all thy doings, and he will direct thee for good; yea, when thou liest down at night lie down unto the Lord, that he may watch over you in your sleep; and when thou risest in the morning let thy heart be full of thanks unto God; and if ye do these things, ye shall be lifted up at the last day."
>
> Alma 37:37

A heart full of thanks is not distracted by what is missing. It is focused on what is present, what is good, and what is eternal. When gratitude fills your heart, it shapes your thoughts, lifts your mood, and strengthens your faith.

This kind of thankfulness doesn't require a perfect life. It only requires a willing heart.

One woman said, "When I made gratitude part of my inner dialogue, I felt more peace. I began noticing joy in ordinary things."

Letting your heart be full of thanks leaves less room for fear and more room for faith.

Today, pause and check in with your heart. What fills it? Invite gratitude to take the lead.

What helps you keep your heart centered in thankfulness throughout the day?

November 28

> *"And whatsoever ye do in word or deed, do all in the name of the Lord Jesus, giving thanks to God and the Father by him."*
>
> Colossians 3:17

Gratitude and charity are closely linked. When your heart is filled with thankfulness, it naturally overflows into love for others. Giving thanks to God transforms how you speak and serve.

Remembering your own blessings makes it easier to share mercy and patience. When you take time to reflect on all the ways God has shown you love, forgiveness, and abundance, it humbles your heart and broadens your compassion. Gratitude softens your judgments and gives rise to generosity and kindness. It shifts your focus from what is lacking to what is possible, from frustration to understanding, and from criticism to care.

One brother said, "When I made a habit of thanking God in everything I did, even in small tasks, I found it easier to be patient and loving with the people around me."

Thankfulness is not only personal. It becomes a gift that blesses everyone you meet.

Today, do one thing in the name of Jesus with a grateful heart, whether in words or deeds, and let it become an offering of love.

In what ways has gratitude helped shape your kindness, patience, or generosity towards others?

November 29

> *"What shall I render unto the Lord for all his benefits toward me?"*
>
> Psalm 116:12

Gratitude often leads to a holy question: *How can I give back to the Lord who has given me everything?* True thanksgiving naturally invites action, a desire to serve, to love, to offer our hearts in return.

The Lord does not need grand gestures. He asks for sincerity, obedience, and love. A grateful soul becomes a giving soul, one that serves naturally because it remembers how deeply it has been blessed. When our hearts are full of thanks, they overflow with compassion.

One sister shared, "I realized that serving others was my way of saying thank you to the Lord. It made service feel more sacred."

Giving back is one way we show that we remember.

Today, ask the Lord how you can offer thanks through action. Serve with a grateful heart.

What can you do today to show your thanks in a way that blesses someone else?

November 30

> *"And he who receiveth all things with thankfulness shall be made glorious; and the things of this earth shall be added unto him, even an hundred fold, yea, more."*
> Doctrine and Covenants 78:19

This promise is not just about the end result. It is about what happens along the way. As you choose to receive all things with gratitude—the joys, the trials, the ordinary—you are refined, lifted, and changed.

That is the glory God promises. It is not found in ease or perfection, but in a heart that trusts Him in all things. It is the quiet radiance of someone who keeps choosing faith, who offers praise in the middle of uncertainty, and who believes that every chapter, both joyful or difficult, can be consecrated for their good.

One young adult said, "Thankfulness made me more open to learning from my struggles. I didn't love the hard moments, but I saw them differently."

Gratitude is the path to spiritual glory.

Today, thank God for one thing you are still learning from. Let it become part of your growth.

How has gratitude helped you become more like Christ, even in hard seasons?

December

Rejoice in Christ, the Light of the world, whose coming brings hope, healing, and everlasting redemption.

December 1

> *"And the angel said unto them, Fear not: for, behold, I bring you good tidings of great joy, which shall be to all people."*
>
> Luke 2:10

THE MESSAGE OF CHRIST'S birth began with joy. From the moment the angel declared His arrival, heaven was inviting the earth to rejoice. That invitation still stands. In every season and circumstance, we are called to find our joy in Him.

Christ's coming means light has entered the world. It means peace is possible, redemption is real, and hope is alive. When you focus on Him, joy becomes more than a fleeting feeling. It becomes a way of living.

One sister said, "When I remember that Jesus came for me, joy feels more personal. It turns the holidays into something holy."

Joy is not found in perfection. It is found in the presence of Christ.

Today, begin this month by rejoicing in the Savior. Let your focus on Him fill your heart with joy.

What brings you joy when you think about the birth of Jesus Christ?

December 2

> *"And we talk of Christ, we rejoice in Christ, we preach of Christ, we prophesy of Christ, and we write according to our prophecies, that our children may know to what source they may look for a remission of their sins."*
>
> 2 Nephi 25:26

To rejoice in Christ is to let Him be at the center of your life. Not just during Christmas, but always. It is to let His love define you, His light guide you, and His promises carry you forward.

This season is not about checking off traditions. It is about remembering why we celebrate. The more you talk of Christ, the more joy you feel in Him. The more you rejoice in Him, the more your heart will be filled with peace.

One brother said, "I made a goal to mention Christ in every conversation this December. It changed the way I experienced the season."

Rejoicing in Christ turns ordinary days into holy ones.

Today, find one way to talk of Christ. Let His name be spoken with love and reverence.

How can you rejoice in Christ more fully as the Christmas season begins?

December 3

> *"Then spake Jesus again unto them, saying, I am the light of the world: he that followeth me shall not walk in darkness, but shall have the light of life."*
>
> John 8:12

Jesus Christ is the light that never dims. In a world filled with uncertainty, distraction, and sorrow, His light cuts through the darkness and shows the way. His light becomes a steady, sure, and sacred part of your life when you choose to follow Him.

Even in quiet moments, His light can fill your soul. It brings comfort to the weary, clarity to the confused, and strength to the faithful.

One young woman said, "I used to feel overwhelmed by everything going wrong in the world. But focusing on Christ brought back my peace. His light gave me perspective."

Light is not the absence of trial. It is the presence of Christ.

Today, seek His light. Let His presence brighten the spaces in your heart that need hope.

Where in your life do you need more of Christ's light?

December 4

> *"For unto us a child is born, unto us a son is given: and the government shall be upon his shoulder: and his name shall be called Wonderful, Counsellor, The mighty God, The everlasting Father, The Prince of Peace."*
> Isaiah 9:6

Each name of Christ reveals something we need. He is Wonderful when you feel forgotten. He is your Counselor when life feels uncertain. He is Mighty when you are weak. He is your Father when you feel alone. He is the Prince of Peace when your heart is heavy.

Rejoicing in Christ means recognizing who He is to you, not just in doctrine, but in daily life. He knows exactly how to meet you where you are and lift you toward where you can be.

One brother said, "When I started praying to know Christ better by His titles, I began to understand His role in my life more personally."

He is everything you need, right now and forever.

Today, choose one name of Christ that you need most. Let that guide your prayers and your thoughts.

Which name or role of the Savior brings you the most comfort today?

December 5

"Behold, I am Jesus Christ, whom the prophets testified shall come into the world. And behold, I am the light and the life of the world; and I have drunk out of that bitter cup which the Father hath given me, and have glorified the Father in taking upon me the sins of the world, in the which I have suffered the will of the Father in all things from the beginning."
3 Nephi 11:10–11

When Christ appeared to the Nephites, He introduced Himself with clarity and love. He declared His mission, His identity, and His role in their salvation. That same introduction speaks to you today. He is your light. He is your life. He is your Redeemer.

Rejoicing in Christ is a deeply personal experience. It means remembering who He is to you as an individual. It means holding on to the truth that He came not only for the world, but for you.

One young adult shared, "I read that verse every December as a reminder of who I'm celebrating. It keeps my focus on Him."

His name is not just a story. It is your source of hope.

Today, read 3 Nephi 11 and reflect on Christ's words. Let His light speak to your heart.

What does it mean to you that Christ is your life and your light?

December 6

> *"Oh, come, let us adore him; Christ, the Lord."*
> O Come, All Ye Faithful, Hymns, no. 202

Adoration is deeper than praise. It is heartfelt reverence, love, and devotion. When you truly adore Christ, it changes how you live. You want to honor Him in your words, your choices, and your priorities. When we turn our hearts towards Christ in adoration, we are filled with a sense of peace, love, and belonging.

This sacred season invites you to slow down and reflect, not just on what Christ has done, but on who He is. Adoration grows as you make time to feel His presence and remember His sacrifice.

One sister said, "Each Christmas I pick one way to 'adore Him' through service or worship. It helps me stay focused on why I celebrate."

Adoring Christ has a profound impact on the human heart, drawing it closer to Him and creating a sense of homecoming. Adoration is not just an act of worship, but a transformative experience that can bring us closer to the divine and fill our hearts with joy and purpose.

Today, find one quiet moment to offer your adoration to the Savior. Let it be sincere and personal.

What does adoring Christ look like in your life right now?

December 7

> *"And the Word was made flesh, and dwelt among us, (and we beheld his glory, the glory as of the only begotten of the Father,) full of grace and truth."*
>
> John 1:14

The wonder of Christmas is God sending his only begotten Son to Earth. Jesus Christ walked among us, felt what we feel, and lived a perfect life so He could redeem ours. His coming was not just symbolic. It was real, personal, and full of purpose.

Rejoicing in Christ means standing in awe of His humility and love. He did not come in grandeur. He came in meekness, so that no one would feel too small to approach Him.

One brother said, "When I picture the Savior choosing to come into this world, not in power but in quiet love, I feel more connected to Him."

The arrival of Christ holds profound significance, symbolizing a new beginning and hope for humanity. One of the most impactful aspects of Christ's arrival is its role in making our homecoming possible.

Today, reflect on what it means that Jesus Christ came to live among us. Let it bring you closer to Him.

What does His choice to dwell with us say about His love for you?

December 8

> *"Glory to God in the highest, and on earth peace, good will toward men."*
>
> Luke 2:14

This angelic message at the Savior's birth was not only an announcement. It was a blessing. The birth of Christ brought peace to a weary world and offered the promise of redemption to every heart.

Peace on earth begins with peace in the heart. That peace is not found in quiet surroundings but in a deep trust in the One who came to save. Christ does not only bring peace. He is peace.

One sister shared, "When I sing that scripture in a Christmas hymn, I try to feel what it meant for heaven to declare peace because He had arrived."

His presence is, without a doubt, the most wonderful and precious gift one could ever receive. His peace is the greatest comfort.

Today, invite the peace of Christ into one area of your life. Ask Him to calm what feels unsettled.

Where do you most need the Savior's peace this season?

December 9

> *"For God so loved the world, that he gave his only begotten Son, that whosoever believeth in him should not perish, but have everlasting life."*
>
> John 3:16

The story of Christ's birth is a story of love. God gave His Son so that you could have hope, healing, and eternal life. Every gift, every tradition, and every act of kindness this season can be a reminder of that first and greatest gift.

When you remember the reason behind it all, your celebrations become more sacred. The love of God is not distant. It is personal, and it was expressed through Jesus Christ.

One young woman shared, "When I think of Christmas as a celebration of God's love for me, everything feels more meaningful. It becomes a time of worship."

The birth of Christ was God's way of telling you that you are never forgotten.

Today, thank your Heavenly Father for the gift of His Son. Let your gratitude become a quiet prayer of love.

How does remembering God's love help you feel closer to Christ during this season?

December 10

> *"He shall feed his flock like a shepherd: he shall gather the lambs with his arm, and carry them in his bosom, and shall gently lead those that are with young."*
>
> Isaiah 40:11

Jesus Christ came not only to save, but to shepherd. He knows how to gather those who are scattered, heal those who are hurting, and carry those who cannot go further on their own. His birth was the beginning of a ministry filled with compassion and care.

To truly rejoice in Christ is to have unwavering faith in His ability to see and meet all of your needs, no matter how great or small they may seem. Even when you are in the midst of your most difficult struggles, know that His gentle guidance is always with you, supporting and leading you through each challenge.

One brother said, "During one of my hardest Decembers, I kept this verse on my fridge. It reminded me that Christ was not just my Savior. He was walking with me."

The Good Shepherd was born to find you.

Today, picture the Savior as your Shepherd. Let Him carry what feels too heavy to bear alone.

What comfort do you find in knowing Christ gathers and carries His sheep with love?

December 11

> *"Come unto me, all ye that labour and are heavy laden, and I will give you rest."*
> Matthew 11:28

The invitation to come unto Christ is not just for those who feel strong. It is especially for those who feel tired, burdened, or unsure. He offers rest that goes deeper than sleep. It is rest for the soul. It is peace that comes from being known, loved, and carried.

During a busy season, it can be easy to feel overwhelmed. But the Savior gently reminds you to come to Him. He does not ask you to be perfect. He asks you to be present.

One sister shared, "When I started bringing my exhaustion to Christ instead of trying to hide it, I felt more peace than I expected."

One cannot find true rest by simply pausing life's activities; rather, true rest is a state of being that transcends the temporal interruptions of a busy schedule. It is found in the presence of the Savior.

Today, let your prayer be simple. Come to Him with what is heavy, and let Him offer His peace.

What does it mean to you that the Savior invites you to rest in Him?

December 12

> *"The Lord is my light and my salvation; whom shall I fear? the Lord is the strength of my life; of whom shall I be afraid?"*
>
> Psalm 27:1

Fear and joy often try to exist in the same space. But where Christ's light is welcomed, fear loses its grip. He is not only your light. He is your salvation. He brings clarity to confusion and courage to the heart.

During this season, as you reflect on the light of Christ, remember that He is with you in the unknowns. He knows the way, and He leads with love.

One young adult said, "When I felt anxious about the future, this scripture reminded me that Christ already saw ahead. That brought me peace."

Rejoicing in and finding joy in Christ means embracing His calming presence, allowing His light to alleviate the burdens of fear and anxiety, fostering a tranquil spirit.

Today, write down a fear and then write how Christ's light can guide you through it. Let Him lead and follow His guidance.

What fear can you surrender to Christ today as you rejoice in His light?

December 13

> *"And she shall bring forth a son, and thou shalt call his name JESUS: for he shall save his people from their sins."*
>
> Matthew 1:21

The name Jesus means "Savior." His very name declares His mission. He did not come just to teach or to heal. He came to save. That truth is the heart of all rejoicing during this season. Because of Him, there is always a way back. There is always hope.

You are one of the people He came to save. That knowledge can bring comfort on hard days and deeper meaning to joyful ones.

One brother said, "When I remember that Jesus came to save me personally, the story of Christmas becomes real. It becomes mine."

His name is not merely a title; it's a symbol of his power, influence, and the expectations placed upon him. It is a promise.

Today, say the name of Jesus with reverence and love. Let it remind you of His personal mission for you.

What does the name Jesus Christ mean to you in this season of rejoicing?

December 14

> *"Verily I say unto you my friends, fear not, let your hearts be comforted; yea, rejoice evermore, and in everything give thanks;"*
> Doctrine and Covenants 98:1

Rejoicing is not only for the easy seasons. It is a way of life rooted in trust and gratitude. When your heart chooses to rejoice, even when things are not simple, you are demonstrating deep faith in the goodness of God.

This kind of rejoicing brings comfort because it is focused on eternal truths rather than temporary troubles. It is a choice to see God's hand and respond with praise.

One young woman said, "I began each morning with three things I was thankful for and one reason to rejoice. It was a transformative experience; that single task had a profound effect and reshaped my whole day from beginning to end.

To rejoice is to believe; to trust that all is well, an act of faith that unlocks the door to inner peace and harmony.

Today, list one reason to rejoice and one thing to be thankful for. Let that frame your thoughts.

How can you choose to rejoice today, no matter what your circumstances look like?

December 15

> *"He hath filled the hungry with good things;
> and the rich he hath sent empty away."*
> Luke 1:53

Mary's words remind us that the Lord sees those who are humble, longing, and open. He fills the hungry, not only those in need of food, but those who hunger for peace, hope, and healing. Christ came for those who recognize their need for Him.

Rejoicing in Christ means coming to Him with a hungry heart. It means being willing to receive what only He can give. It also means trusting that His gifts will satisfy the deepest parts of your soul.

One sister said, "When I stopped trying to fill my heart with distractions and turned to Christ, I felt truly full."

He still fills the hungry with good things. That promise is as true today as it was then.

Today, ask the Lord to fill you with what He knows you truly need. Come to Him with a willing heart.

What are you hungry for that only Christ can provide?

December 16

> "And now, after the many testimonies which have been given of him, this is the testimony, last of all, which we give of him: That he lives!"
>
> Doctrine and Covenants 76:22

Christmas is not only about remembering a birth. It is about rejoicing in a living Savior. Jesus Christ came, lived, died, and rose again. Because He lives, there is reason to hope, to change, and to keep going. His life gives meaning to ours.

Rejoicing in Christ includes bearing testimony of Him. It may be through words, actions, or quiet conviction. However you share it, the truth remains—He lives.

One brother said, "When I bear testimony of Christ, I feel closer to Him. I feel His reality more deeply. I am grateful for this deepening connection and look forward to continuing to nurture and strengthen my relationship with Him."

Your testimony of Christ is one of the most sacred gifts you can offer.

Today, bear simple testimony of the Savior in a prayer, journal, or conversation. Let your heart rejoice in His reality.

What helps you feel and share your testimony that Jesus Christ lives?

December 17

> *"And the Spirit and the bride say, Come. And let him that heareth say, Come. And let him that is athirst come. And whosoever will, let him take the water of life freely."*
>
> Revelation 22:17

The invitation to come unto Christ is extended to all. It is for those who are thirsty for truth, tired from the journey, or simply longing for more peace. The Savior invites you to come without hesitation, no matter where you are on the path.

This is the heart of the gospel message. Christ does not wait for you to be perfect. He calls to you as you are, offering living water to those who seek Him.

One young woman said, "When I finally believed the invitation was meant for me personally, everything changed. I felt His love for real."

There is room for everyone at the feet of Jesus. Even the most burdened, the most broken, find solace in His boundless compassion.

Today, accept the invitation to come unto Christ in one small way. Let Him meet you where you are.

What does it mean to you to be invited personally by the Savior?

December 18

> *"And the light shineth in darkness; and the darkness comprehended it not."*
>
> John 1:5

Light does not eliminate all darkness at once, but it always shines. The Savior came into a world filled with confusion and pain, and His light still shines. No matter how dark things may feel, the light of Christ is stronger.

Rejoicing in Christ means holding to that light. It means choosing to see with hope when fear tries to settle in. The darkness may not understand the light, but it cannot overcome it. Faith in the Savior, is not a passive acceptance, but an active defiance of the shadows. It's the unwavering belief that even in the deepest night, dawn will break, and we can be saved through His light.

One brother said, "When I choose to focus on the Savior, even for a few moments, the weight I carry feels lighter."

Christ is the Light that never fades. His radiance, a beacon in the darkest night, guides our steps toward eternity.

Today, spend time with a scripture or message that brings you spiritual light. Let it lift you.

Where have you seen the Savior's light overcome darkness in your life?

December 19

> *"Peace I leave with you, my peace I give unto you: not as the world giveth, give I unto you. Let not your heart be troubled, neither let it be afraid."*
>
> John 14:27

The peace of Christ is different from what the world offers. It does not depend on perfect circumstances or a quiet environment. His peace can calm a troubled heart in the middle of noise, sorrow, or uncertainty. It is a gift meant to be felt, trusted, and shared.

Rejoicing in Christ means receiving His peace with gratitude. It means believing that He will carry you through and calm you within.

One sister said, "The more I trusted His peace, the less I needed everything around me to be fixed. His presence was enough."

Christ's peace is not fragile. It is steady, personal, and powerful.

Today, invite His peace into one area of your life where there is tension. Let it settle your heart.

How has the peace of Christ helped you move forward with calm and courage?

December 20

> *"For the Son of man is come to seek and to save that which was lost."*
>
> Luke 19:10

The reason we rejoice is simple. He did not come just to teach or inspire, but to redeem. His birth marked the beginning of a rescue mission meant for every soul willing to receive Him—including you.

There is no sin too great, no heart too broken, no past too far gone. Jesus Christ came to heal and restore. His saving power is personal, and His grace is real.

One brother shared, "When I finally accepted that Christ wanted to save me, not just others, I found real joy. His love became deeply personal, and He began guiding me every day."

Jesus Christ came with a specific purpose in mind, *to bring salvation and redemption to all humanity*. His ultimate mission was to offer forgiveness for sins and to bridge the gap between God and mankind. Embracing the message of Jesus Christ can bring hope, peace, and eternal life to those who believe in him.

Today, reflect on how Christ has saved you personally. Let that fill your heart with gratitude.

In what ways have you felt the saving power of Jesus Christ in your life?

December 21

"For with God nothing shall be impossible."
Luke 1:37

This verse was spoken to Mary by the angel who declared she would be the mother of the Son of God. It was a message of reassurance, not just for her, but for all who believe. With God, even the most unexpected promises can be fulfilled. Even the most unlikely paths can lead to miracles.

Rejoicing in Christ means trusting in the God of the impossible. This isn't simply a passive acceptance; it's an active, unwavering faith in a power that transcends human understanding and limitations. It means believing that His power, the very power that created the universe and raised Jesus from the dead, is greater than any fear, anxiety, or doubt that may assail us. It's a belief that surpasses the limitations of our human perspective, acknowledging that His strength is made perfect in our weakness.

One young adult said, "When I face things that feel impossible, I come back to this verse. It reminds me that I am not alone, and God still works miracles."

Faith makes room for the impossible to become possible.

Today, write down one thing that feels impossible and give it to God in prayer. Trust Him with it.

What would change in your life if you truly believed that nothing is impossible with God?

December 22

> *"And the Word was made flesh, and dwelt among us, (and we beheld his glory, the glory as of the only begotten of the Father,) full of grace and truth."*
>
> John 1:14

The miracle of Christ's birth is more than a moment in history. It is a testimony of divine love of God. Jesus Christ came to dwell with us so He could lift us, heal us, and lead us back to our Father. He came full of grace for your shortcomings and truth for your confusion.

To rejoice in Christ is to rejoice in the nearness of God. You are not left alone to figure life out. The Savior came to walk with you, speak to you, and carry you.

One sister said, "When I think of Jesus not just coming to the earth but choosing to dwell among us, I feel closer to Him. He really understands."

He came close so you could draw near. The act of coming close symbolizes a gesture of kindness and empathy. In a world where distance and detachment often prevail, the simple act of coming close can be a powerful reminder of the importance of connection and understanding.

Today, reflect on what it means that Christ came to dwell with us. Thank Him for His nearness and love.

How does knowing Christ is near help you rejoice even in difficult times?

December 23

> *"The next day John seeth Jesus coming unto him, and saith, Behold the Lamb of God, which taketh away the sin of the world."*
> John 1:29

The Savior was born in humility, but His mission was eternal. He came not just to be adored in a manger, but to atone for all sin. Every part of His life pointed to His role as the *Lamb of God*. That is why we rejoice. Because of Him, there is redemption. Because of Him, there is hope.

As you reflect on the birth of Jesus Christ, remember His purpose. He did not come to condemn. He came to save, to lift, and to change hearts forever. His presence brings salvation, healing, and lasting change to the heart and soul.

One brother said, "When I remember that the baby in Bethlehem became the *Lamb of God*, my gratitude deepens. It reminds me that His love came with a purpose."

Rejoicing in Christ means receiving the gift of His Atonement with a grateful heart.

Today, take a moment to thank the Savior for His sacrifice. Let your love for Him grow deeper.

What does it mean to you that Christ came to take away your sins?

December 24

> *"For unto you is born this day in the city of David a Saviour, which is Christ the Lord."*
> Luke 2:11

The night Christ was born was quiet and holy. Yet the impact of that moment echoes through eternity. A Savior was given to the world, not just to one people or place, but to all. He is your Savior, personally and completely.

Tonight, let the quiet message of Christmas settle in your heart. You have a Redeemer. He came willingly, lived perfectly, and loves you endlessly. His birth is not just a story from long ago, it is a living reminder of God's mercy and His plan for your peace. The greatest gift has already been given. He came wrapped in swaddling clothes, full of grace and truth.

One sister said, "Christmas Eve always reminds me to pause. To breathe. To remember that Jesus came for me, and that is worth celebrating. That gentle reminder brings clarity in a season that can feel rushed or distracted. It brings stillness to a world that rarely slows down."

Today, spend a few quiet minutes reflecting on the birth of Christ. Let that joy fill your home and heart.

What helps you keep Christ at the center of your Christmas Eve worship?

December 25

> *"Behold, a virgin shall be with child, and shall bring forth a son, and they shall call his name Emmanuel, which being interpreted is, God with us."*
>
> Matthew 1:23

The wonder of Christmas is captured in one name—Emmanuel. God with us. Not far away or unreachable, but near. Present. Personal.

On this holy day, we celebrate more than a baby in a manger. We celebrate the miracle of Jesus Christ, who came to dwell among us. He walked our roads, bore our griefs, and offered us redemption. His birth fulfilled prophecy, changed the course of history, and opened the door for each of us to come home to God.

Christmas is a reminder that we are never alone. In our loneliness, Christ is with us. In our joy, He rejoices with us. In our sorrow, He strengthens us. The presence of the Savior is the greatest gift ever given, and He gives Himself freely to all who seek Him.

One sister said, "This year I read the nativity story by candlelight before opening a single gift. I felt like I was honoring Christ as my first gift of the day."

Today, pause and offer a heartfelt prayer of worship. Thank the Lord for coming. Invite Him to stay.

How will you honor the Savior's presence in your life this Christmas?

December 26

> *"But as many as received him, to them gave he power to become the sons of God, even to them that believe on his name:"*
>
> John 1:12

The day after Christmas can feel quiet. The wrapping is cleared, the songs are softer, and the pace begins to slow. But the gift remains alive. Christ is not just a memory of a holy night. He is a present, living Savior who continues to bless us every day.

In His birth we receive more than forgiveness. We receive a new identity. Believing and accepting Jesus carries us into His family. We become sons and daughters of God.

Let gratitude shine beyond the season. Rejoicing in Christ goes far past a date on the calendar. It shapes a lifetime, reminding us that our worth and belonging come from Him rather than our achievements.

One young man said, "After Christmas, I remind myself that the gift of Jesus did not end. He is still with me. Every day, I live as one of His children."

Gratitude keeps the joy of Christ alive in your heart and confirms your place in His family.

Today, offer a prayer of thanks for the gift of your new identity in Christ. Let that gratitude carry into the new year.

How can you carry the spirit of Christmas into the days that follow?

December 27

"Let your light so shine before men, that they may see your good works, and glorify your Father which is in heaven."

Matthew 5:16

As the year draws to a close, we're reminded that our lives are meant to reflect the Savior. His light within us is not just for personal comfort. It is meant to shine out through kindness, integrity, and Christlike actions.

Your daily discipleship is a cornerstone of rejoicing in Christ. Every act of service, every gentle word, every moment spent in prayer is a flicker of His light shining in the world. These small, consistent choices testify of Jesus and inspire others to glorify God.

One woman said, "I want to carry the spirit of Christ into every season. If I keep rejoicing in Him, that spirit stays with me."

Rejoicing in Christ is not a seasonal event. It is a lifelong way of living, with light, faith, and love guiding your steps.

Today, look for a simple way to shine. Perhaps with a kind word, a small act of service, or sharing a gospel thought. Let your light be noticed.

How can you continue to reflect Christ's light into the coming year?

December 28

> *"... I am come that they might have life, and that they might have it more abundantly."*
> John 10:10

The life Christ offers is full of purpose, joy, and hope. It does not mean every day will be easy. But it does mean you are never without strength, direction, or peace. He came so that your life could be filled with more light than you could find on your own.

Rejoicing in Christ includes embracing the abundant life He invites you to live. That abundance comes through grace, growth, and the constant companionship of His Spirit.

One brother said, "I realized that living abundantly meant living with Christ. When I include Him in everything, life becomes more meaningful."

True abundance is found in walking with the Savior, where peace is deeper than circumstance, joy is rooted in eternal truth, and love flows freely regardless of the world around you.

Today, thank the Lord for the abundant life He offers. Look for one way to live it more fully.

What does an abundant life in Christ look like for you right now?

December 29

"Wherefore, lift up thy heart and rejoice, and cleave unto the covenants which thou hast made."

Doctrine and Covenants 25:13

Joy in Christ is not separate from commitment. It is found within it. When you hold to your covenants with sincerity and love, you feel a closeness to the Savior that brings peace and strength. Rejoicing in Him is not only about remembering. It is also about choosing to walk in His way.

Your covenants are a source of joy because they connect you to His promises. They remind you of who you are and who you are becoming in Him.

One sister shared, "Every time I renew my covenants, I feel a quiet joy. It reminds me that He is always near."

Joy grows when you stay close to Christ through your covenants. As you remember Him, honor your promises, and live by His word, your heart begins to change. His Spirit becomes more constant, and even in trials, you feel anchored in hope and purpose.

Today, reflect on a covenant you have made. Ask the Lord to help you rejoice more fully in it.

How does your commitment to Christ bring lasting joy to your life?

December 30

> *"And now, my beloved brethren, I would that ye should come unto Christ, who is the Holy One of Israel, and partake of his salvation, and the power of his redemption. Yea, come unto him, and offer your whole souls as an offering unto him, and continue in fasting and praying, and endure to the end; and as the Lord liveth ye will be saved."*
>
> Omni 1:26

At the heart of rejoicing in Christ is this invitation: *come to Him and receive what He alone can give.* Salvation, redemption, and peace are not earned. They are offered freely through His grace. You only need to come.

This is not a one-time decision. It is a daily return. Each time you turn to the Savior, you partake of His goodness again. That is where rejoicing begins.

One young woman said, "Even when I fall short, I know I can always come back to Christ. That brings me more hope than anything else."

The joy of redemption is never out of reach.

Today, come to Christ again in prayer or scripture. Let your heart rejoice in His power to redeem.

What does partaking of Christ's redemption mean to you today?

December 31

> *"O my sons, I would that ye should remember that these sayings are true, and also that these records are true. And behold, also the plates of Nephi, which contain the records and the sayings of our fathers from the time they left Jerusalem until now, and they are true; and we can know of their surety because we have them before our eyes."*
>
> Mosiah 1:6

As the year comes to a close, it is a sacred time to look back and remember. Remember the moments the Lord spoke peace to your heart. Remember the prayers He answered, the strength He gave, and the ways He carried you when you felt too tired to go on.

Rejoicing in Christ means trusting that what He has done, He will continue to do. He does not change. His love, mercy, and promises remain as true today as they were at the beginning of the year.

One sister shared, "I make a list each New Year's Eve of the ways Christ has been present in my life. It helps me walk into the next year with more faith."

Gratitude for the past builds faith for the future.

Today, write down three ways you have seen the hand of the Lord this year. Thank Him for walking with you.

How has your relationship with Jesus Christ grown over the past year?

About the Author

Emmaline Hoffmeister is a devoted disciple of Jesus Christ, a covenant-keeping woman of faith, and a writer who delights in bringing light to everyday moments. With a deep love for scripture and a heart anchored in the gospel of Jesus Christ, she writes to inspire reflection, peace, and personal connection with the Savior.

Her devotional work is rooted in the belief that spiritual strength is built daily, that holiness is found not only in quiet reverence, but in laundry rooms, traffic jams, and every act of love and obedience. Each word she writes is prayerfully crafted to uplift, encourage, and draw others closer to Christ.

After years of writing award-winning fiction, this volume marks Emmaline's tenth published book and her first devotional book. It is a deeply personal offering, born of study, prayer, and her own desire to walk more closely with the Lord. She considers it both a labor of love and an act of discipleship. Emmaline enjoys helping others recognize the Lord's hand in their own lives. She believes in miracles, lives by grace, and seeks the Spirit in all things.

Emmaline holds degrees in accounting and psychology from Central Washington University and Brigham Young University–Idaho. She spent 12 years working as a fraud investigator and as an accountability, legal compliance, financial, and performance auditor before choosing to become a stay-at-home mom. She launched her writing and publishing career in 2009, writing in the Regency Romance genre. Her latest Christian fiction novel, *Left Behind*, received the *Eternal Perspective Christian Literary Award* from the Northwest Faith & Fiction Award Committee.

A lover of story, structure, and scenic places, Emmaline's creativity is shaped by her travels and by the rugged beauty of the many places where she has lived with her husband and two (now grown) sons.

Visit emmalinehoffmeister.com to view her full portfolio of books.

www.ingramcontent.com/pod-product-compliance
Lightning Source LLC
Chambersburg PA
CBHW011408070526
44586CB00022B/2597